BRITAIN'S Royal NATIONAL THEATRE
the first 25 years

Written and compiled by Tim Goodwin

Edited by **John Goodwin** and **Lyn Haill** (Assistant **Liz Curry**)
Designed by **Michael Mayhew** (Assistant **Samantha Dumiak**)
Stephen Wood did much of the picture research

Published by the National Theatre in association with Nick Hern Books
Nick Hern Books is a division of Walker Books Limited, 87 Vauxhall Walk, London SE11 5HJ

Printed by **Battley Brothers**, Clapham, London SW4 0JN
Set in **Rockwell** and **Helvetica**

British Library Cataloguing in Publication Data
Britain's Royal National Theatre: The first twenty-five years.
1. Great Britain. National theatres. National Theatre (Great Britain), to 1988
I. Goodwin, Tim II. National Theatre (*Great Britain*)
792'.0941

ISBN 1-85459-005-7 Pbk
1-85459-070-7 Hbk

Cover: typography and layout, **Richard Bird**.
Front cover: from the setting for the NT's 1988 productions of *The Winter's Tale, The Tempest* and *Cymbeline* designed by **Alison Chitty**; photograph, **John Haynes**.
Back cover: Peter Hall and Laurence Olivier in 1973 when Hall succeeded Olivier as Director of the National Theatre; photograph, BBC Hulton Picture Library.
Inside covers: most of these posters were designed by Richard Bird, and many either by him and Michael Mayhew together, or by Michael Mayhew alone; Tom Phillips designed the poster "The New National Theatre is Yours"

The National Theatre company began life on 22 October 1963 – the date they opened in the Old Vic, taking it over as a temporary base until their permanent home on the South Bank was completed.

For the next twelve-and-a-half years, whilst waiting to occupy their own much-delayed theatre, virtually all the company's productions were staged at the Old Vic.

Then, in March 1976, came the move to the South Bank. This took place before the building was finished, despite the difficulties, in order to make a start there. Performances were given in the Lyttelton, the only auditorium of the NT's three that was ready. The other two opened to the public as they became usable: the Olivier in October 1976, the Cottesloe in March 1977.

By the time the company reached their 25th anniversary, in October 1988, and since their move to the South Bank alone, they had won 134 major drama awards, a record. But this book does not attempt a critical appraisal of the work over 25 years. It is intended as a celebration of an historic birthday.

It everywhere aims to be as comprehensive as the format of the book allows. But with the Production Scrapbook, the largest part, it has been necessary to simplify and to reduce the huge amount of relevant material.

Even so, three hundred and four productions are listed in the Scrapbook: the total number (apart from the exceptions mentioned below) that the NT has given on its main stages over the 25 years. But there is only room for pictures of fewer than a quarter of these productions. Those chosen, 68 in all, were selected because they were either remarkable box-office successes, or remarkable critical successes, or both.

Sunday night performances, platform performances, occasional workshops, and studio nights could not be recorded in the Scrapbook because of pressure on space; nor, for the same reason, could regional tours, which from the South Bank averaged 16 weeks each year; nor tours overseas; nor transfers of NT productions to the West End.

The cast lists and dates are as at a production's first NT performance. The terminology is as printed in the original programmes.

JG

CONTENTS

BEGINNINGS

From the first idea to the foundation of
the NT company at the Old Vic

The heart of the Elizabethan theatre of Shakespeare, Marlowe, Jonson and their contemporaries – the golden age of English drama – was in London, on the South Bank of the River Thames, and it is here, appropriately, that the National Theatre of Great Britain has been built.

Several European countries have had national theatres for two or even three centuries, theatres set up on the order of absolute monarchs, the enlightened despots of the time. In contrast British money was earmarked for trade, not national prestige, or the arts.

The first firm plan for a British National Theatre was put forward in 1848. Effingham Wilson, "the Radical Bookseller of the Royal Exchange", issued a couple of pamphlets suggesting "a house for Shakespeare" in public ownership, where the works of the "world's greatest moral teacher" would be constantly performed.

Little more happened until 40 years later, when the great actor-manager, Henry Irving, attempted to turn the Lyceum Theatre into a *de facto* National Theatre by staging a mixture of modern plays and large-cast theatrical classics, with top stars. But the venture collapsed into bankruptcy, despite critical acclaim and full houses.

Pressure for a National Theatre increased enormously with the publication in 1907 of a book by the critic William Archer, and

Above: Henry Irving in *The Bells*
Right: Harley Granville Barker

Harley Granville Barker, a young director-actor-author. *The National Theatre: A Scheme and Estimates* covered everything from staff and repertoire to wages, royalties and pension funds. The company were to total 66 (44 men and 22 women), seats would cost 1 shilling to 7/6d (5p to 37½p) and the entire scheme was expected to cost a third of a million pounds. The artistic establishment rallied to support the plan. Writers like Barrie, Galsworthy, Pinero and Shaw joined actors, critics, and social and political leaders. The Shakespeare Memorial National Theatre Committee was established in 1908 to raise the necessary money, as state aid was assumed to be out of the question.

The idea quickly became so fashionable, few doubted the reality would soon follow. Even the opening date of the unbuilt building was set – 23 April 1916, the tercentenary of Shakespeare's death. In 1913 a private member's Bill to establish a National Theatre got a small majority in the House of Commons, and a site was bought in Gower Street, Bloomsbury. When the First World War broke out the following year, a hut was built there to provide entertainment for wounded soldiers, but, as the years went by, nothing else. The possibility of a National Theatre threatened to disappear.

Eventually, in 1930, Granville Barker issued a new edition of his and Archer's book, urging two theatres under one roof, and a site on the

Below: The Duchess of Wellington's Quadrille Party: one of the many events to raise funds for a National Theatre

Shakespeare Memorial National Trust

Left: Bernard Shaw presenting the symbolic twig and piece of earth to Geoffrey Whitworth, then secretary of the National Theatre Committee
Below: Lilian Baylis

BBC Hulton Picture Library

South Bank of the Thames, between Westminster and Waterloo Bridges. But the Great Depression was not a good time to expect people to listen. Nevertheless the campaign did not cease, and a new site was bought in 1937, in Cromwell Gardens, opposite the Victoria and Albert Museum. A design for the theatre was drawn up by Edwin Lutyens, and Bernard Shaw presided over 'The Ceremony of the Twig and the Sod' to the accompaniment of Old English madrigals sung by the Fleet Street choir. A year later, war again exploded across Europe. Surprisingly, the long-term effect of the Second World War was beneficial to the idea of a National Theatre.

State aid for the arts was introduced in 1940 and CEMA (Council for the Encouragement of Music and the Arts), the forerunner of the Arts Council, was founded. The National Theatre land in Cromwell Gardens (used as a water tank for fire engines during the Blitz) was exchanged for a London County Council site in their planned redevelopment of the South Bank. Then, towards the end of the war, a vital ally joined the National Theatre cause: the Old Vic organisation. This was the creation of Lilian Baylis whom Peter Hall describes in his *Diaries* as "that strange, Cockney, busybodying, straight-laced, crooked-mouthed eternal mother, bossing every-body about''.

In 1898 the 24-year-old Lilian Baylis had begun to help her aunt, Emma Cons, who managed the Royal Victoria Hall and Coffee Tavern in the Waterloo Road, the ''Old Vic''. Here the working classes of south London were provided with morally uplifting entertainment, including theatre. In 1912 Lilian Baylis became the manager herself and, with single-minded determination, set about turning the Old Vic into the home of Shakespeare and opera in London. In 1931 she acquired Sadler's Wells, for staging opera and ballet. By 1937, when she died, Lilian Baylis had laid the foundations not only for the National Theatre, but for the Royal Ballet and the English National Opera. In 1944 the Old Vic company were run by a triumvirate of Laurence Olivier, Ralph Richardson and John Burrell. On tour, and at the New Theatre, a series of legendary productions were staged, including Olivier's performance as

Michael Boys

Above: Kenneth Tynan (*left*) and Richard Findlater stage a mock funeral at the NT foundation stone – now in the Lyttelton foyer – to protest at the apparent death of a dream
Below: Ruskin Spear's painting of Ralph Richardson as Falstaff
Left: Laurence Olivier as Richard III

Above: Lord Chandos, Chairman of the NT Board 1963-1971
Below: Laurence Olivier as Astrov in Chekhov's *Uncle Vanya*

Richard III and Richardson's as Falstaff. The chance seemed to have come to create a National Theatre company, even before a theatre had been built.

The post-war Chancellor of the Exchequer, Sir Stafford Cripps, promised that, if the necessary legislation was passed by Parliament, the Treasury would contribute up to a million pounds towards the building of a National Theatre. In 1949 the National Theatre Bill was passed without a vote. Everything looked rosy but, not for the first time, nor the last, matters came to a grinding halt as Britain slid into financial crisis.

Two years later the then Queen Elizabeth, mother of the present Queen, laid a foundation stone, specially dedicated by the Archbishop of Canterbury. There was no particular likelihood of a theatre to follow, nor did one. As politicians prevaricated and the planned National Theatre site was repeatedly changed, the foundation stone was shuttled up and down the South Bank. The Queen Mother was reported to have suggested the stone be put on castors. In 1961 the Chancellor, Selwyn Lloyd, seemed to kill all hopes of a National Theatre by stating publicly that the money needed to build it would not be found.

Paradoxically, this attempt to bury the National Theatre raised it to life. The theatrical profession combined with the Arts Council to protest vigorously at the government's denial of its legal responsibilities. Shortly after, the London County Council offered to pay part of the cost of construction – now estimated at £2 to 3 million – and provide the site rent-free. The government hastily back-tracked and agreed to contribute the money promised in 1949.

Next year the National Theatre Board was set up under Oliver Lyttelton, followed by the South Bank National Theatre and Opera House Board, which would oversee building work. But there had been sites and boards before. This time, though, the freshly-rediscovered enthusiasm would be given an irresistible impetus.

Laurence Olivier, then Director of the Festival Theatre at Chichester, was appointed Director of the National Theatre in 1962, and a company were assembled at Chichester. Rather than wait for a new building, the National Theatre company gave their first performance at the Old Vic on 22 October 1963. It was as well they did not wait. The NT building was still 12½ years away.

Angus McBean

NATIONAL RECORD 1963 TO 1988

a chronology of key events

1963

22 October. At their temporary home, the Old Vic, the National Theatre Company under Laurence Olivier give their first-ever performance, the uncut *Hamlet*, directed by Olivier, with Peter O'Toole in the name part. The repertoire also includes Chekhov's *Uncle Vanya*, a transfer from Chichester Festival Theatre, with Michael Redgrave and Laurence Olivier, and Farquhar's *The Recruiting Officer*.

Denys Lasdun is chosen as the architect of the National Theatre building. For two years he explores the problem, helped by Laurence Olivier and a committee of nine directors (Michael Benthall, Peter Brook, Michel St. Denis, George Devine, John Dexter, Frank Dunlop, Michael Elliott, William Gaskill and Peter Hall); four designers (Roger Furse, Jocelyn Herbert, Sean Kenny, Tanya Moiseiwitsch); a lighting designer (Richard Pilbrow); a manager (Stephen Arlen); and an actor (Robert Stephens). Kenneth Tynan, literary manager of the National Theatre, is also consulted.

Below: Peter O'Toole as Hamlet
Below right: The Old Vic

Angus McBean

The Guardian

1964

A ticket for Laurence Olivier's towering performance in *Othello* is described by the *Daily Express* as "the most difficult piece of paper to get hold of in Britain today." Peter Shaffer's epic *The Royal Hunt of the Sun* is the NT's first world premiere. The Compagnia Proclemer-Albertazzi from Italy, in *Hamlet*, are the first foreign visitors.

1965

The NT company go to Russia. Olivier's *Othello* is an enormous success there, and Peter Wood's production of Congreve's *Love For Love* has its first performance in the Kremlevsky Theatre, Moscow, within the walls of the Kremlin. Meanwhile the Berliner Ensemble from East Berlin take over the Old Vic in three of Brecht's plays – *The Resistible Rise of Arturo Ui, The Days of the Commune*, and *The Threepenny Opera* – and in Brecht's adaptation of Shakespeare's *Coriolanus*. Other visitors are the Théâtre du Nouvel Monde from Canada and the National Youth Theatre.

It is estimated that the National Theatre will cost £5½ million to build, and the South Bank Opera House, then planned as its companion, another £4 million.

1966

The NT company go £250,000 into the red. Jennie Lee, the Arts Minister, announces an increase in the government subsidy to cover the deficit.

Jacques Charon comes over from the Comédie Française to direct John Mortimer's adaptation of Feydeau's *A Flea in Her Ear*. The NT company expand into the Queen's Theatre in the West End to present a ten-week season of their work.

1967

Rising costs cause a drastic rethink of the National Theatre building scheme. The opera house part of it is abandoned (the Sadler's Wells Company, scheduled to be housed there, eventually move to the Coliseum to become the English National Opera). The site of the National Theatre is moved yet again, but for the last time.

Kenneth Tynan, the NT's literary manager, wants the NT to put on Rolf Hochhuth's *Soldiers*. The play portrays Winston Churchill as

Olivier defends
The Soldiers
'BAN' ROW O
CHURCHILL PL
PLAY ABOUT CHURCHILL REJEC
Stand
and fight,
Sir Laurence

Top: The Berliner Ensemble at the end of *Coriolanus* at the Old Vic
Above: Some headlines from the *Soldiers* controversy
Right: Jennie Lee, and then GLC Leader Desmond Plummer, give a ceremonial start to building work on the National Theatre

being involved in the 'assassination' of the Polish anti-communist leader, General Sikorski, who died in an air crash in 1943. Pressure from the NT Board, led by its then Chairman, Lord Chandos, who as Oliver Lyttelton was a member of Churchill's wartime cabinet, stops the play being done at the Old Vic. Later it is produced by other companies.

A new play, *Rosencrantz and Guildenstern are Dead* makes the name of Tom Stoppard. When asked what the play is about, Stoppard replies "It's about to make me very rich."

1968
The NT makes a profit, but only with the help of further increased subsidies and by cutting the number of new productions. Clifford Williams directs a controversial, but successful, all-male *As You Like It*. John Gielgud joins the NT company to act in Molière's *Tartuffe* and Seneca's *Oedipus*. The latter, in an adaptation by the poet, Ted Hughes, is directed by Peter Brook, his only NT production to date.

1969
An amendment to the National Theatre Act 1949 authorises increased government expenditure of up to £3,750,000 on building and equipping the National Theatre. This amount is to be matched by the GLC (formerly London County Council). With the money guaranteed, work starts on the building at last. A ceremonial cement-pouring marks the beginning of construction. Shovels are wielded by Jennie Lee, Lord Chandos, Lord Cottesloe (Chairman of the South Bank Board and ex-Chairman of the Arts Council), and Desmond Plummer (leader of the GLC).

Despite Olivier's doubts, Peter Nichols's *The National Health* provides a success for new NT director Michael Blakemore, and is later made into a major film. The Compagnie Renaud-Barrault from France visits with *Rabelais* adapted by Jean-Louis Barrault. The NT mounts a season of experimental work at the Jeannetta Cochrane Theatre.

1970
Money from recent surpluses is used to finance the Young Vic, a converted building on the Waterloo Road which, from now and until it is incorporated as a separate company in 1973, serves the NT as

a studio theatre, run by Frank Dunlop. The Young Vic opens with *Scapino*, Dunlop's own version of Molière's *Les Fourberies de Scapin*.

Ingmar Bergman directs a non-Scandinavian company for the first time – the NT company in Ibsen's *Hedda Gabler*, a production which Olivier called "one of the great prides of my time at the National." Olivier's Shylock in *The Merchant of Venice* also brings in the crowds. The Cambridge Theatre is taken over for a 30-week season of NT productions. With plays on at the Old Vic, the Young Vic, and the Cambridge, the NT has its first experience of running three theatres at once.

Companies from the Nottingham Playhouse and Abbey Theatre, Dublin visit the Old Vic.

Laurence Olivier becomes the first actor ever to be created a life peer.

1971

Work on the National Theatre building is delayed by a labour shortage and rising costs. The opening date is pushed back from 1973 to 1974. Lord Chandos retires as Chairman of the National Theatre Board and is succeeded by Sir Max Rayne, created Lord Rayne in 1976.

Olivier takes on his last-but-one major stage role – James Tyrone in O'Neill's *A Long Day's Journey Into Night*. Paul Scofield joins the NT for a year; his most notable performance is in Zuckmayer's *The Captain of Köpenick*. The New Theatre (now the Albery) is taken over for a season, but this is not a success. The Young Vic makes an award-winning tour of Europe.

Visitors to the Old Vic include the Belgium National Theatre with Michel de Ghelderode's *Pantagleize* and Dario Fo's *The Seventh Commandment*, and companies from the Octagon Theatre, Bolton, and the Theatre Royal, York. Guest directors include Victor Garcia from Spain who directs Arrabal's *The Architect and the Emperor of Assyria*, and Manfred Wekwerth and Joachim Tenschert from East Germany who direct Shakespeare's *Coriolanus*.

Godfrey Argent

1972

Ford's *'Tis Pity She's A Whore* is the NT's first mobile production, touring small venues and colleges. Four more mobile productions are done over the next 2½ years. Main house successes include a new Tom Stoppard play *Jumpers* (with Michael Hordern and Diana Rigg), and Hecht and MacArthur's comedy about the press, *The Front Page*, which subsequently plays a season in Australia.

1973

The National Theatre and Museums of London Bill becomes law, providing another £2 million for construction. The oil crisis causes a huge rise in energy costs, sharply forcing up the costs of building the new National Theatre, and of maintaining it when open. The new building is 'topped out' by Laurence Olivier and Lord Cottesloe.

Olivier gives his last stage performance to date, as the veteran Trotskyist, John Tagg, in Trevor Griffiths' *The Party*. Franco Zeffirelli visits the Old Vic to direct Eduardo de Filippo's *Saturday, Sunday, Monday*. Peter Shaffer returns with another success, *Equus*, directed (as was *The Royal Hunt of The Sun*) by John Dexter, who also directs Molière's *The Misanthrope*. This is translated by the poet Tony Harrison, and marks the start of a strong link between him and the NT.

Below left: Lord Rayne, then Sir Max Rayne, Chairman of the NT Board 1971-1988
Below: Laurence Olivier as John Tagg in *The Party* – his last stage role
Below right: Lord Cottesloe and Laurence Olivier at the National Theatre's "topping out" ceremony

John Haynes

Zoë Dominic

Nobby Clark

Above: Laurence Olivier, John Gielgud,
Ralph Richardson, Peggy Ashcroft, Peter Hall
celebrate Gielgud's 70th birthday
Left: Laurence Olivier
Right: Laurence Olivier in the NT's temporary offices –
the huts in Aquinas Street
Below: Susan Fleetwood (Sybil Thorndike) and Peggy
Ashcroft (Lilian Baylis) rehearse *A Tribute to the Lady* –
the last NT performance at the Old Vic
Below right: Albert Finney as Hamlet (poster designed
by Richard Bird and Michael Mayhew)

Nobby Clark

Keystone Press

HAMLET

William Shakespeare

Olivier resigns as Director because of ill health, to be succeeded by Peter Hall. The opening of the new building is put back again, to 23 April (Shakespeare's birthday) 1975.

1974

Building difficulties continue. Work on the wiring is several months behind. Other problems surround installing and testing the newly-designed stage equipment. The opening is delayed further. The National Theatre Bill 1974 removes the limit on government support for the building work.

The NT production of Wedekind's *Spring Awakening*, directed by Bill Bryden, causes controversy because of a scene involving masturbation. Trevor Griffiths' *Comedians*, directed by Richard Eyre, visits the Old Vic from Nottingham Playhouse.

1975

Ralph Richardson and John Gielgud act together in Harold Pinter's *No Man's Land*, directed by Peter Hall. It is one of several new plays written specially for the opening of the NT, and subsequently transfers to the West End, to New York, and to the Lyttelton Theatre when the new building opens.

It is decided to move into the still-unfinished building and open it theatre by theatre, as each nears completion, rather than wait any longer. The NT staff leave the temporary huts in Aquinas Street, which have served as their offices throughout the company's time at the Old Vic, and start work in the new building. *Hamlet* is rehearsed on the Lyttelton stage.

1976

On 28 February comes the last NT performance after 12 years at the Old Vic, Val May's *A Tribute to the Lady*, a documentary about Lilian Baylis with Peggy Ashcroft as Lilian Baylis. Hall describes it as "one of the finest performances I have seen her give."

8 March: Peggy Ashcroft in Beckett's *Happy Days* begins a week of previews in the Lyttelton Theatre of transfers from the Old Vic. Other transfers are J. M. Synge's *The Playboy of the Western World*, Ben Travers's *Plunder*, Ibsen's *John Gabriel Borkman*, John Osborne's *Watch It Come Down* (specially written for the NT opening), and *Hamlet*.

The Lyttelton Theatre officially opens on 16 March, with the uncut

Hamlet, directed by Peter Hall, with Albert Finney as Hamlet.

Ralph Richardson inaugurates Ralph's Rocket, which was fired before every NT first night. Another play specially written for the NT opening – *Weapons Of Happiness* by Howard Brenton – is put on in the summer.

The first NT platform performance is staged – *Scenes from National Life*. Since then over 1500 of these short, early evening performances have been given in one or other of the building's three theatres. They range from poetry readings to short plays, discussions and even conjuring shows. Among the people to appear have been the poets Tony Harrison, Seamus Heaney, Philip Larkin, and Yevgeny Yevtushenko; playwrights Alan Ayckbourn, Alan Bennett, Howard Brenton, Athol Fugard, Christopher Hampton, Arthur Miller and Arnold Wesker; Peter Brook; and the composer Harrison Birtwistle.

Foyer music begins – free live concerts ranging from baroque and jazz to folk, are given by professional groups every evening in the Lyttelton foyer before performances.

The first exhibitions are put up in the NT foyer – *A Language and a Theme: The Work of Denys Lasdun and Partners*; and *British Stage Designers*. Since then well over 200 exhibitions have been shown, ranging from the works of Ernst Dryden, Angus McBean and Ralph Steadman to the *Spitting Image* puppets and the Yiddish Theatre of London's East End.

The Olivier Theatre, delayed still further by industrial troubles,

Tony Russell

Above: Ralph Richardson lights Ralph's Rocket
Below left: Tamburlaine on the terraces. Albert Finney (Tamburlaine) is in the straw hat
Above right: Lord Rayne, The Queen, and the Duke of Edinburgh at the Royal Opening of the National Theatre
Below right: Part of *The Passion* – the Crucifixion – is performed on the terraces for Easter

Nobby Clark

Nobby Clark

eventually opens on 4 October. The production is Marlowe's 4¾-hour-long *Tamburlaine The Great*, directed by Peter Hall, with Albert Finney in the name part. Before then, long excerpts from the production had been performed outside on the terraces, free, to passers-by.

The building is officially opened by The Queen on 25 October, with productions of Goldoni's *Il Campiello* in the Olivier – a critical disaster – and, in the Lyttelton, a revival of Tom Stoppard's *Jumpers*. The building is still far from finished.

The Théâtre National Populaire from Lyon, France, visit the Lyttelton in Molière's *Tartuffe*, directed by Roger Planchon, and Marivaux's *La Dispute*, directed by Patrice Chéreau.

1977

The National Theatre finally becomes fully operational with the opening of the Cottesloe Theatre on 4 March. The first production is Ken Campbell and Chris Langham's *Illuminatus!* an 8½-hour epic by the Science Fiction Theatre of Liverpool.

The total cost of building the NT is £16 million.

The Crucifixion is performed outside on the terraces for Easter Saturday. It is part of *The Passion*, a selection from the York Mystery Plays, written by Tony Harrison and the actors, and directed by Bill Bryden and Sebastian Graham-Jones. Over the next eight years this will grow into a particular NT triumph, *The Mysteries*, a three-play cycle that moves from the Creation to

Nobby Clark

Doomsday, staged as a promenade production with the action taking place around and amongst the audience.

A strike breaks out over the dismissal of a plumber, Ralph Cooper, for failing to fix two wash-basins. It lasts six days.

Maximilian Schell comes to the NT to direct Ödön von Horváth's *Tales from the Vienna Woods*, translated by Christopher Hampton. Paul Scofield returns in, among other parts, the title role in Jonson's *Volpone*. Three more plays written for the NT opening produced: Alan Ayckbourn's *Bedroom Farce*, a record-breaking success and subsequently televised; Robert Bolt's *State Of Revolution*; and Stephen Poliakoff's *Strawberry Fields*. The NT gives its first Christmas show for children, *Sir Gawain and the Green Knight*, adapted by Peter Stevens and directed by Michael Bogdanov. Backstage areas are opened to the public for NT Tours. (Tours of the building have remained constantly popular and now take place about 20 times a week.)

Visiting productions from overseas are Gorki's *Summerfolk* by the Schaubühne from West Berlin, directed by Peter Stein, and Ramon del Valle Inclán's *Divinas Palabras* by the Nuria Espert Company from Spain, directed by Victor Garcia. Visiting productions from Britain include the Phoenix Theatre Leicester; the Birmingham Repertory Theatre; the Manchester Library Theatre; Stephen Berkoff's London Theatre Group; the English Stage Company; Moving Being Theatre Company; and Paine's Plough.

Mozart's *Don Giovanni*, in Peter Hall's Glyndebourne production, is presented for six performances in the Lyttelton – an experiment. It packs, but the acoustics are not yet thought ideal for opera.

A financial crisis breaks. The NT is £500,000 in the red due to construction delays and the discovery that the building costs over £1 million a year to run before anything is put on its stages. A special government grant comes to the rescue, but the NT can no longer afford to present visiting companies.

1978

Bill Bryden and Sebastian Graham-Jones direct another promenade production, Keith Dewhurst's *Lark Rise*, a dramatisation of Flora Thompson's book *Lark Rise to Candleford*.

Edward Bond's *The Woman*, David Hare's *Plenty*, and Harold

Above: NATTKE members meet outside the NT during a strike
Below: Two of the many newspaper cartoons about *The Romans in Britain* scandal

"*Of course, we were terribly lucky with the notices.*"

Pinter's *Betrayal* are premiered at the NT. The last two are later made into major films.

The Baylis Terrace is opened. It is named after Lilian Baylis who, in her 25 years running the Old Vic (1912 to 37) laid the foundations of the National Theatre, the English National Opera, and the Royal Ballet.

An overtime ban by stage staff and unofficial strikes over pay disrupt the theatre.

1979

An unofficial strike over pay and work shifts by backstage staff in March completely closes all the NT's three theatres. Among the plays affected is John Galsworthy's *Strife*, about a strike in a Welsh tin-plate works. *Strife* and some other productions are put on again, but in either the wrong or limited decor. Three weeks later, following many attempts at negotiation, the NT is forced to dismiss the 70 strikers. A demonstration and a scuffle interrupt one performance. Over the next two months the strike gradually fades away, having cost the NT over a quarter of a million pounds.

Tom Stoppard's adaptation of Schnitzler's *Undiscovered Country* features John Wood and Dorothy Tutin, and especially spectacular settings by William Dudley, including a working hotel lift.

Warren Mitchell (TV's Alf Garnett) wins three best actor awards as Willy Loman in Michael Rudman's production of Arthur Miller's *Death of a Salesman*.

Peter Shaffer's new play *Amadeus*, directed by Peter Hall in the Olivier, becomes, at this date the most successful NT production ever. It wins 13 top awards, goes on to enjoy runs in London's West End and New York, and the play is later made into an Oscar-winning film.

1980

Athol Fugard brings his play *A Lesson From Aloes* from the Market Theatre, Johannesburg, to the Cottesloe Theatre. (Later – in 1983 – he also brings his next play *Master Harold . . . and the Boys*, to the Cottesloe and, subsequently, the Lyttelton.)

The premiere of Howard Brenton's *The Romans In Britain* causes an uproar. The scene where a Roman soldier attempts the homosexual rape of a druid results in a private prosecution for obscenity being brought against the play's director, Michael Bogdanov, by Mary Whitehouse. But the case is not to come to trial until March 1982.

A performance of Ibsen's *The Wild Duck* is interrupted when the duck begins quacking. Bill Bryden directs O'Neill's five-hour marathon *The Iceman Cometh*, as part of his extensive NT work on 20th-century American plays. John Dexter's production of Brecht's *The Life of Galileo* is a special triumph for Michael Gambon as Galileo. Michael Bogdanov's adaptation of Longfellow's *Hiawatha* is put on as a Christmas show for children. It is so popular it is revived several times, and becomes the NT's first national tour for children.

1981

Peter Hall's long-planned production of the world's earliest dramatic masterpiece, *The Oresteia* trilogy by Aeschylus, is finally staged to great acclaim. It is done with full masks and an all-male cast, in a version by Tony Harrison with music by Harrison Birtwistle. The production is filmed for TV by the newly-established Channel 4.

Shaw's *Man and Superman*, directed by Christopher Morahan, is presented in its full form, including the almost invariably cut *Don Juan in Hell* scene. Michael Bogdanov's production of Calderon's *The Mayor of Zalamea* becomes the first Cottesloe show to transfer to the Olivier. John Schlesinger directs Sam Shepard's *True West*, with Bob Hoskins and Antony Sher.

Stevie Wonder gives an impromptu late-night concert in the Lyttelton foyer after attending the NT's *Measure for Measure*, given by a mainly black cast, and directed by Michael Rudman.

1982

The Oresteia is taken to Greece and performed in the ancient classical theatre at Epidaurus, which seats 15,000, making the NT the first British company to perform a Greek play in Greece.

The private prosecution of *The Romans in Britain* director, Michael Bogdanov, is brought to trial at the Old Bailey amidst a storm of media coverage. After three days the prosecution is dropped and *nolle prosequi* entered on the record.

The enormous success of Richard Eyre's production of *Guys and*

Nobby Clark

Dolls enables the NT temporarily to withstand cuts in real terms in the Arts Council's grant. The musical wins 11 awards, brings new audiences to the NT, and runs for nearly 750 performances, first in the Olivier and then in the West End.

Richard Eyre also directs John Gay's *The Beggar's Opera*. Peter Hall directs Wilde's *The Importance of Being Earnest* and Harold Pinter's new play *A Kind of Alaska*. Alan Ayckbourn's *Way Upstream* is put on in the Lyttelton, with a real cabin cruiser sailing in a huge tank of water. Technical problems and flooding when the tank is punctured provide much good copy for Fleet Street and cost several performances.

An anonymous donor enables the NT to give a series of Bargain Nights with all tickets costing only £2 each. The first Bargain Night is a performance of *Guys and Dolls*. The scheme continues for each production over 14 months.

The NT Education Department sends out to about 20 towns and cities its first production, Brecht's *Caucasian Chalk Circle*. This has no conventional costumes, sets, or props, but uses whatever each venue provides. Since then the Education Department has staged ten more productions, ranging from Shakespeare to contemporary writers and one-man shows.

1983

The publication of *Peter Hall's Diaries*, giving a unique view of what it is like to run Britain's National Theatre, causes a stir.

The NT produces a second major musical, this time a new one, *Jean Seberg*, composer Marvin Hamlisch, lyricist Christopher Adler, dramatist Julian Barry. The production, by Peter Hall, is dogged with problems, is badly received, and does not run long.

Ralph Richardson, who is performing for the NT in Eduardo de Filippo's *Inner Voices*, dies aged 81.

Peter Wood directs Sheridan's *The Rivals* with particular success. Other well-received NT productions include the premiere of Christopher Hampton's *Tales from Hollywood*, and of David Mamet's *Glengarry Glen Ross*, which transfers from the Cottesloe to the Mermaid Theatre.

1984

A second opera from Glyndebourne is put on in the Lyttelton,

Knussen and Sendak's *Where The Wild Things Are*, which draws crowds of children.

A number of different actors' groups are formed within the framework of the NT – a system which continues to the end of Peter Hall's regime. The groups led by Alan Ayckbourn, and Ian McKellen and Edward Petherbridge, are particularly successful.

Financial troubles rise up again because of the continuing failure of the Arts Council grant to keep pace with inflation, and the NT suffers its first deficit for six years.

The NT wins many awards, particularly for Chekhov's *Wild Honey*, adapted by Michael Frayn, and Shakespeare's *Coriolanus*, both with Ian McKellen in the leading role, and a Sam Shepard play, *Fool for Love*.

The NT Studio is founded. It is run by Peter Gill, financed by private sources, and housed in the Old Vic annexe, leased rent-free by Ed Mirvish. It provides the NT company with the chance to refine and extend their skills, and also generates new writing and experimental work. Regular studio nights take place in the Cottesloe when examples of work-in-progress are shown to the public for one night only.

John Haynes

1985

The steadily worsening financial position forces the NT to close down the Cottesloe – the last performance is *Doomsday*. Bill Bryden's production of *The Mysteries* cycle, of which *Doomsday* is a part, transfers to the Lyceum, the first live theatre to be staged there for over 30 years.

At a hurriedly-called press conference, Peter Hall climbs onto a coffee table to make sure he can be seen and heard, and makes a sensational attack on government cut-backs in the arts.

The NT has a series of hits, with Hare and Brenton's new play *Pravda* – called "the hottest ticket in London" by several US newspapers; Alan Ayckbourn's *A Chorus of Disapproval*, now a film; and Chekhov's *The Cherry Orchard*, directed by Mike Alfreds and part of the work of the group of actors led by Ian McKellen and Edward Petherbridge. *Coriolanus* is performed in the huge Herodes Atticos Theatre in Athens, built by the Romans in AD 161 just beneath the Parthenon.

Nobby Clark

Left: Peter Gill rehearsing in the NT Studio
Below left: William Dudley (left) the designer of
The Mysteries; Bill Bryden (centre) the director;
and Tony Harrison, the author, at rehearsals
Right: Peter Hall and Ian McKellen in the Roman
amphitheatre at Athens, before a performance of
Coriolanus

In the autumn the Cottesloe re-opens thanks to a special grant
from the soon-to-be-abolished GLC. Peter Gill puts on a festival of
ten new plays there.

The NT receives 20 major awards for its year's work.

1986

George Orwell's *Animal Farm*, adapted and directed by Peter Hall,
becomes the first production to play in all the NT's three theatres.
It also tours widely in Britain and abroad. Eastern bloc pressure
stops it being performed in the programme of an international
theatre festival in Baltimore USA. It is finally staged there, but not
as part of the festival.

Brecht and Weill's *The Threepenny Opera* is the first main-house NT
production to be sponsored – by Citicorp/Citibank. Previously
sponsorship had been sought only for studio and educational work,
foyer music, platform performances, exhibitions and so on.

Neil Simon has a play put on at the NT for the first time, *Brighton
Beach Memoirs*, directed by Michael Rudman. The NT's Christmas
show is *The Pied Piper* by Adrian Mitchell, devised and directed by

Alan Cohen, with music by Dominic Muldowney. In the cast are children from many different schools playing rats; the play is revived the next year.

David Hare directs *King Lear*. Anthony Hopkins, as Lear, gives 100 performances of the part – a record.

The NT tours abroad more than ever before, including visits to France, Austria, Switzerland, the USA and Canada.

1987

Private sponsorship enables the NT to present an International Theatre Festival. The visitors are the Schaubühne from West Germany with O'Neill's *The Hairy Ape*, directed by Peter Stein; the Royal Dramatic Theatre Company from Sweden with Ingmar Bergman's productions of *Hamlet* and Strindberg's *Miss Julie*; the Ninagawa Company from Japan with *Macbeth* and Euripides' *Medea*; and the Mayakovsky Theatre from Moscow with Boris Vasiliev's *Tomorrow Was War*. The Market Theatre of Johannesburg also comes to the NT in Percy Mtwa's *Bopha!*.

A party and entertainment are given in the Olivier to celebrate Laurence Olivier's 80th birthday.

The NT receives a record 22 major awards for its year's work. Major successes include Arthur Miller's *A View from the Bridge*, with Michael Gambon as Eddie Carbone; Shakespeare's *Antony and Cleopatra* with Anthony Hopkins and Judi Dench; Alan Ayckbourn's *A Small Family Business*; Peter Gill's new play *Mean Tears*; Beckett's *Waiting for Godot* with Alec McCowen and John Alderton; and David Edgar's *Entertaining Strangers,* first staged by Ann Jellicoe with the people of Dorchester.

1988

Peter Hall directs three of Shakespeare's late plays – *The Winter's Tale, The Tempest* and *Cymbeline* – his last productions as Director of the NT. They are put on in the Cottesloe as part of the Endgames Festival – a South Bank celebration of late work. The Late Shakespeares later visit the USSR and Japan, and transfer to the Olivier.

Tennessee Williams' *Cat on a Hot Tin Roof* has its first major revival since its British premiere in 1958, when it was banned by the Lord

Michael Carter

Below: The company for the Late Shakespeares outside the Moscow Art Theatre, 1988
Right: Peter Hall

John Haynes

Chamberlain and could only be given by turning the Comedy Theatre into a private club. It is Howard Davies' first production for the NT and is a big critical and popular success. His production of Boucicault's *The Shaughraun* – also enthusiastically received – uses the lift mechanism of the NT's drum revolve for the first time since the revolve was installed in 1976.

Richard Eyre directs Middleton and Rowley's *The Changeling* – his first production as the NT's Director-designate.

From its 25th birthday in October, The Queen approves the title of Royal for the National Theatre, in recognition of its achievements.

Richard Eyre succeeds Peter Hall in September as Director of the National Theatre, with David Aukin as Executive Director. Some weeks earlier they unveil plans for the next 12 months.

Lord Rayne retires as Chairman of the NT Board in December, to be succeeded by Lady Soames.

Below: Richard Eyre rehearsing *The Changeling*
Below centre: David Aukin
Below right: Lady Soames, Chairman of the NT Board from 1989

John Haynes

John Haynes

Universal Pictorial Press Agency

PRODUCTION SCRAPBOOK 1963 TO 1988

a choice of NT successes year by year
in pictures: with comment and complete cast lists

1963

UNCLE VANYA
by **Anton Chekhov**, trans.
by **Constance Garnett**

CAST: Wynne Clark *(Marina Timofeyevna)*, Laurence Olivier *(Mihail Lvovitch Astrov)*, Michael Redgrave *(Ivan Petrovitch Voynitsky – Uncle Vanya)* Max Adrian *(Alexander Vladimirovitch Serebryakov)*, Keith Marsh *(Ilya Ilyitch Telyegin – Waffles)* Joan Plowright *(Sofya Alexandrovna – Sonya)* Rosemary Harris *(Ilyena Andreyevna)*, Enid Lorimer *(Marya Vassilyevna Voynitsky – Maman)* Robert Lang *(Yefim)* *Production by* Laurence Olivier, *Designed by* Sean Kenny, *Costumes by* Beatrice Dawson, *Guitar music arranged by* Alexis Chesniakov, *Lighting by* John Read

Angus McBean

Right: **Michael Redgrave** (Vanya),
Joan Plowright (Sonya)

❝When the 'phone call came from Larry Olivier suggesting *Uncle Vanya* for the opening season at the Chichester Festival in 1961, I said yes at once. Rehearsals began in a drill hall behind Sloane Square. "I know you think there's no such thing as a definitive performance, but this . . ." Larry murmured in my ear at the first reading, as he closed the book on the last page. It was rumoured that he had insured the Festival against loss, and looking about one at the cast he had assembled for *Vanya* I thought What an insurance! Joan Plowright, Sybil Thorndike and Lewis Casson, Joan Greenwood, André Morrell, Peter Woodthorpe and Larry himself as Astrov . . .
I thought his Astrov faultless, I wished fervently that Mother could have lived to see our *Uncle Vanya* . . . Antony and Vanya are the two performances I am proudest of.❞
Michael Redgrave *(In my Mind's Eye)*

❝*Uncle Vanya* was simply the best English Chekhov – maybe the best classic production and certainly the greatest feast of acting – ever. Michael Redgrave's Vanya was an incomparable tragi-comic creation, a portrait of failure that made the spectator ache with recognition.❞
Robert Cushman
(The National Theatre at The Old Vic 1963-1971)

All the plays that opened in 1963:

HAMLET by William Shakespeare, Dir. Laurence Olivier, Old Vic 22.10.63
SAINT JOAN by Bernard Shaw, Dir. John Dexter, Old Vic 30.10.63

UNCLE VANYA by Anton Chekhov, trans. by Constance Garnett, Dir. Laurence Olivier, Old Vic 19.11.63
THE RECRUITING OFFICER by George Farquhar, Dir. William Gaskill, Old Vic 10.12.63

The Recruiting Officer is based on Farquhar's first-hand experience while recruiting in Shrewsbury. Within the conventional framework of a Restoration comedy, he set down his own detailed observation of the effect of a recruiting campaign on a small country town. There are no longer recruiting campaigns, conscription has been abolished, and war is now in the hands of scientists and politicians. What is the particular compulsion for us today of the image of a group of soldiers arriving in a country town? I think what we recognise from our experience is the systematic deception of the ignorant to a pointless end by the use of heroic images of the past, a past no longer relevant. We may laugh at the recruits but we recognise our own plight.

William Gaskill *(NT's programme)*

The Recruiting Officer is really a play within a play within a play, and Gaskill has pared layer after layer of this brilliant satire with the dexterity of a neurosurgeon. He peers beneath the surface and takes his audience with him as he probes into the hidden recesses of the play . . . *The Recruiting Officer* is the most brilliant production I have ever seen on any English stage.

Jacob Siskind *(Montreal Star)*

Lewis Morley

1963 THE RECRUITING OFFICER
by George Farquhar

CAST: Anthony Nicholls *(Mr Balance)*, Peter Cellier *(Mr Scale)*, Michael Turner *(Mr Scruple)*, Derek Jacobi *(Mr Worthy)*, Robert Stephens *(Captain Plume)*, Robert Lang *(Captain Brazen)*, Colin Blakely *(Kite)*, James Mellor *(Bullock)*, John Stride *(Costar Pearmain)*, Keith Marsh *(Thomas Appletree)*, Michael Rothwell *(Bridewell)*, Robert Russell *(Pluck)*, Dan Meaden *(Thomas)*, Clive Rust *(A Poacher)*, Michael Byrne *(A Collier)*, Alan Ridgway *(Drummer)*, Christopher Chittell *(Boy with whistle)*, Bruce Purchase *(Balance's steward)*, Michael Gambon *(Melinda's servant)*, Sarah Miles *(Melinda)*, Maggie Smith *(Silvia)*, Jeanne Hepple *(Lucy)*, Lynn Redgrave *(Rose)*, Barbara Hicks *(Poacher's wife)*, Elizabeth Burger *(Collier's wife)*
Production by William Gaskill, *Scenery and costumes by* Rene Allio, *Music arranged by* Richard Hampton

Left: **Maggie Smith** (Silvia), **Lynn Redgrave** (Rose)

1964

OTHELLO
by William Shakespeare

CAST: Michael Rothwell *(Roderigo),* Frank Finlay *(Iago),* Martin Boddey *(Brabantio),* Laurence Olivier *(Othello),* Derek Jacobi *(Cassio),* Edward Petherbridge, George Innes, *(Senate Officers),* Edward Caddick *(Gratiano),* Kenneth Mackintosh *(Lodovico),* Harry Lomax *(Duke of Venice),* Terence Knapp *(Duke's officer),* Keith Marsh *(Senator),* Tom Kempinski *(Sailor),* Peter John *(Messenger),* Maggie Smith *(Desdemona),* Edward Hardwicke *(Montano),* William Hobbs, Roger Heathcott, Keith Marsh, *(Cypriot officers),* Joyce Redman *(Emilia),* Neil Fitzpatrick *(Herald),* Mary Miller *(Bianca),* Raymond Clarke, Neil Fitzpatrick, Reginald Green, Roger Heathcott, William Hobbs, George Innes, Caroline John, Peter John, Tom Kempinski, Terence Knapp, Keith Marsh, Ron Pember, Edward Petherbridge, Sheila Reid, John Rogers, Robert Russell, Frank Wylie *(Senators, Soldiers, Cypriots) Production by* John Dexter, *Scenery and costumes by* Jocelyn Herbert, *assisted by* Suzanne Glannister, *Lighting by* Leonard Tucker, *Music arranged by* Richard Hampton, *Fights arranged by* William Hobbs

Right: **Laurence Olivier** (Othello),
Maggie Smith (Desdemona)

❛God Almighty, I don't know why I chose to do Othello. . . .❜
Laurence Olivier *(Life Magazine)*

❛The last speech was spoken kneeling on the bed, her body clutched upright to him as a shield for the dagger he turns on himself. As he slumped beside her on the sheets, the current stopped . . . We had seen history, and it was over.❜
Ronald Bryden *(New Statesman)*

❛The audience from the back of the theatre swept down the central gangway in a great human tide. They stood three deep in front of the stage, hurling flowers and clapping, many with their hands above their heads. But two rows in front of me I saw a woman in black – sitting while all around her were on their feet, crying "Bravo!" What was the matter? Was she anti-Shakespeare? Anti-British? A Russian critic perhaps? Then she turned slightly and I saw. Tears were running down her cheeks.❜
Felix Barker *(Evening News) from Moscow, where this* Othello *was given, September 1964*

❛An anthology of everything that has been discovered about acting in the last three centuries. It's grand and majestic, but it's also modern and realistic. I would call it a lesson for us all.❜
Franco Zeffirelli

All the plays that opened in 1964:

HOBSON'S CHOICE by Harold Brighouse, Dir. John Dexter, Old Vic 7.1.64
ANDORRA by Max Frisch, trans. by Michael Bullock, Dir. Lindsay Anderson, Old Vic 28.1.64

PLAY by Samuel Beckett, Dir. George Devine, and
PHILOCTETES by Sophocles, adapted by Keith Johnstone, Dir. William Gaskill, Old Vic 7.4.64
OTHELLO by William Shakespeare, Dir. John Dexter, Old Vic 21.4.64

THE MASTER BUILDER by Henrik Ibsen, adapted by Emlyn Williams, Dir. Peter Wood, Old Vic 9.6.64
THE DUTCH COURTESAN by John Marston, Dir. William Gaskill and Piers Haggard, Old Vic 13.10.64

Colin Blakely (Pizarro), **Robert Stephens** (Atahuallpa)

Angus McBean

CAST: Robert Lang *(Martin Ruiz)*, Roy Holder *(Martin Ruiz as a boy)*, Colin Blakely *(Francisco Pizarro)*, Michael Turner *(Hernando de Soto)*, James Mellor *(Fray Vincente de Valverde)*, Michael Gambon *(Diego de Trujillo)*, Dan Meaden *(Salinas)*, Trevor Martin *(Rodas)*, Robert Russell *(Vasca)*, Tom Kempinski *(Domingo)*, Christopher Timothy *(Juan Chavez)*, Derek Jacobi *(Felipillo)*, Kenneth Mackintosh *(Fray Marcos de Nizza)*, Frank Wylie *(Pedro de Candia)*, Peter Cellier *(Miguel Estete)*, Robert Stephens *(Atahuallpa)*, Edward Petherbridge *(Villac Umu)*, Edward Hardwicke *(Callcuchima)*, Neil Fitzpatrick *(Manco)*, Peter John *(Chieftain)*, Bruce Purchase *(Headman)*, Louise Purnell *(Inti Coussi)*, Caroline John *(Oello)*
Michael Byrne, Christopher Chittell, Nicholas Edmett, Terence Knapp, Ron Pember, Alan Ridgway, Clive Rust, Pauline Taylor *(Peruvian Indians)*
Musicians: Alan Cumberland, Roy Jones, Edward Joory, Anne Collis
Production by John Dexter and Desmond O'Donovan, *Scenery and costumes* by Michael Annals, *Music and sound effects* by Marc Wilkinson, *Movement* Claude Chagrin, *Lighting* Brian Freeland

1964 THE ROYAL HUNT OF THE SUN
by Peter Shaffer

❝Why did I write *The Royal Hunt*? To make colour? Yes. To make a spectacle? Yes. To make magic? Yes – if the word isn't too debased to convey the kind of excitement I believed could still be created out of "total" theatre.❞
Peter Shaffer

❝I do not think the English stage has been so graced since Shaw was in his heyday half a century ago.❞
Bernard Levin (Daily Mail)

❝Woven deep into the glittering almost musical comedy fabric of this National Theatre extravaganza is the personal relationship between General Francisco Pizarro and Atahuallpa, Sovereign Inca of Peru. In these two men is posed the eternal problem of conqueror and victim, Christianity and paganism, the new order and the barbaric simplicity of the old. No solution is offered, only pessimism and grief and pain at man's incapacity to live with his brother.❞
Herbert Kretzmer (Daily Express)

❝A second visit to Mr. Shaffer's astonishing play confirms all my first impressions and provokes many more. And they all add up to the finest new play I have ever seen. Mr Shaffer has taken the conquest and destruction of the mighty Inca kingdom of Peru by a handful of Spaniards under Pizarro, and from this seed of story have sprung a thousand flowers of theme.❞
Bernard Levin (Daily Mail)

HAY FEVER by Noël Coward, Dir. Noël Coward,
Old Vic 27.10.64
THE ROYAL HUNT OF THE SUN by Peter Shaffer,
Dir. John Dexter and Desmond O'Donovan,
Old Vic 8.12.64

1965

LOVE FOR LOVE
by William Congreve

CAST: Anthony Nicholls *(Sir Sampson Legend)*, John Stride *(Valentine)*, Robert Lang *(Scandal)*, Laurence Olivier *(Tattle)*, Albert Finney *(Ben)*, Miles Malleson *(Foresight)*, Tom Kempinski *(Jeremy)*, Harry Lomax *(Trapland)*, Michael Gambon *(Snap)*, Keith Marsh *(Buckram)*, Reginald Green *(Servant to Sir Sampson)*, David Hargreaves *(Servant to Foresight)*, Roy Holder *(Blackamoor)*, Edward Hardwicke *(Robin)*, Leonard Whiting *(Singer)*, Geraldine McEwan *(Angelica)*, Madge Ryan *(Mrs Foresight)*, Joyce Redman *(Mrs Frail)*, Lynn Redgrave *(Miss Prue)*, Barbara Hicks *(Nurse to Miss Prue)*, Janina Faye *(Jenny)*
Petronella Barker, Anne Godley, Michael Gambon, Edward Hardwicke, William Hobbs, Roy Holder, Anthony Hopkins, Lewis Jones, Sheila Reid, Malcolm Reynolds, Maggie Riley, Malcolm Terris, Christopher Timothy, Leonard Whiting *(Sailors, Women, Servants etc.)*
Production by Peter Wood, *Designs by* Lila de Nobili, *Music by* Marc Wilkinson, *Dances by* Alfred Rodrigues, *Lighting by* Richard Pilbrow

❛It is still for me one of the finest comedies in the language.❜
Peter Wood (from the programme for the NT's revival in 1985)

❛Peter Wood's production of *Love for Love* aims successfully at stressing the play's social relevance. Firm, money-based establishment is the underlying principle of all these characters. What little there is of warmth and humanity in Congreve is made the most of: the result is a riot of incidental delight.❜
J. W. Lambert (Sunday Times)

❛I've said twice before in these pages that this production seems as near faultless as any I can call to mind. I still think so. I laughed as much last night as I laughed on my previous visits, I delighted as much in the colour of Lila de Nobili's costumes and sets, I enjoyed the way in which the music and the dances are dovetailed in. When Olivier's Tattle realises he has married the wrong woman (Joyce Redman's delicious Mrs Frail) he still makes me weep with laughing when he gives his agonised cry, "I never liked anybody less in my life!" Great acting, great direction, great play.❜
B. A. Young (Financial Times)

Below: **Tom Kempinski** (Jeremy), **Joyce Redman** (Mrs Frail), **Colin Blakely** (Ben), **Anthony Nicholls** (Sir Sampson), **Madge Ryan** (Mrs Foresight), **Laurence Olivier** (Tattle), **Miles Malleson** (Foresight), **Lynn Redgrave** (Miss Prue), **Malcolm Terris** (Servant), **Barbara Hicks** (Nurse), **Geraldine McEwan** (Angelica), **John Stride** (Valentine), **Robert Lang** (Scandal)

Zoe Dominic

All the plays that opened in 1965:

THE CRUCIBLE by Arthur Miller, Dir. Laurence Olivier, Old Vic 19.1.65
MUCH ADO ABOUT NOTHING by William Shakespeare, Dir. Franco Zeffirelli, Old Vic 16.2.65

MOTHER COURAGE AND HER CHILDREN by Bertolt Brecht, trans. by Eric Bentley, lyrics trans. by W. H. Auden, music by Paul Dessau, Dir. William Gaskill, Old Vic 12.5.65
ARMSTRONG'S LAST GOODNIGHT by John Arden, Devised by John Dexter and William Gaskill, Proscenium Production Albert Finney, Old Vic 12.10.65

LOVE FOR LOVE by William Congreve, Dir. Peter Wood, Old Vic 20.10.65
TRELAWNY OF THE WELLS by Arthur W. Pinero, Dir. Desmond O'Donovan, Old Vic 17.11.65

Zoë Dominic

1966

A FLEA IN HER EAR
by Georges Feydeau,
trans. by John Mortimer

CAST: Edward Hardwicke (Camille Chandebise), Sheila Reid (Antoinette Plucheux), Robert Lang (Etienne Plucheux), Kenneth Mackintosh (Dr Finache), Anne Godley (Lucienne Homenides de Histangua), Geraldine McEwan (Raymonde Chandebise), Albert Finney (Victor Emmanuel Chandebise), John Stride (Romain Tournel), Frank Wylie (Carlos Homenides de Histangua), Petronella Barker (Eugenie), Michael Turner (Augustin Ferraillon), Margo Cunningham (Olympe), Keith Marsh (Baptistin), Peter Cellier (Herr Schwarz), Albert Finney (Poche)
Janie Booth, David Hargreaves, Lewis Jones, Maggie Riley, Christopher Timothy (Guests at the Hotel Coq d'Or)
Musicians: Henry Krein, Nigel Pinkett, John Reid
Production by Jacques Charon, Designs by Andre Levasseur, Lighting by John B Read

Left: **Albert Finney** (Poche),
Geraldine McEwan (Raymonde Chandebise)

It is a practical impossibility to condense the plot of a Feydeau farce. His world is a world that spins forward in a headlong rush of episode and incident, gathering steadily in hysteria, rapidity and momentum as the narrative proceeds in and out of innumerable doors, open windows, cupboards, closets, and under sumptuous beds in shady houses. No incident is introduced arbitrarily. The whole edifice is held together by an implacable logic. Played by a company as expert as that of Britain's National Theatre, the result is a delight and an amazement.
Herbert Kretzmer (Daily Express)

There is, of course, a staircase; there are also four doors and an outer exit. But, most important, there is a pivoted wall with a bed on each side, so that at the pressure of a button, it swings round time after time, usually with the wrong occupant (or occupants). Everybody in the cast, without exception, is netted in the mesh of the plot.
J. C. Trewin (Birmingham Post)

All the plays that opened in 1966:

A FLEA IN HER EAR by Georges Feydeau, trans. by John Mortimer, Dir. Jacques Charon, Old Vic 8.2.66

MISS JULIE by August Strindberg, trans. by Michael Meyer, Dir. Michael Elliott, and
BLACK COMEDY by Peter Shaffer, Dir. John Dexter, Old Vic 8.3.66
JUNO AND THE PAYCOCK by Sean O'Casey, Dir. Laurence Olivier, Old Vic 26.4.66

A BOND HONOURED by John Osborne (based on Lope de Vega), Dir. John Dexter, presented with *Black Comedy* (as above), Old Vic 6.6.66
THE STORM by Alexander Ostrovsky, adapted by Doris Lessing, Dir. John Dexter, Old Vic 18.10.66

1967

ROSENCRANTZ AND GUILDENSTERN ARE DEAD
by Tom Stoppard

CAST: John Stride *(Rosencrantz)*, Edward Petherbridge *(Guildenstern)*, Graham Crowden *(The Player)*, Alan Adams, Oliver Cotton,) Neil Fitzpatrick, Luke Hardy,) Roger Kemp *(Players)*, John McEnery *(Hamlet)*, Caroline John *(Ophelia)*, Kenneth Mackintosh *(Claudius)*, Mary Griffiths *(Gertrude)*, Peter Cellier *(Polonius)*, David Bailie *(Fortinbras)*, David Hargreaves *(Horatio)*, David Ryall *(Ambassador)*
David Bailie, Petronella Barker, David Belcher, Margo Cunningham, Denis de Marne, Kay Gallie, Reginald Green, David Hargreaves, William Hobbs, Richard Kay, Lee Menzies, Lennard Pearce, Ron Pember, Frederick Pyne, Maggie Riley, David Ryall, Christopher Timothy *(Courtiers and attendants)*
Player musicians: Lawrence Kennedy, Laurie Morgan, Stephen Nagy
Offstage musicians: Malcolm Hall, Edward Wilson
Production by Derek Goldby, *Designed by* Desmond Heeley, *Lighting by* Richard Pilbrow, *Music and sound effects by* Marc Wilkinson, *Mime by* Claude Chagrin

Right: **John Stride** (Rosencrantz), **Edward Petherbridge** (Guildenstern)

❝A cobwebbed, weed-choked Gothic palace descends around them from the skies. A rotting, crewless ship of death rises from under their feet. Some complex and dangerous drama is in progress somewhere just around the next backdrop. Kings and queens and plotters and pirates rush off and on, a glowing, glittering pack of playing-card enigmas, mysterious principals in some lavish, sinister, dressy pantomime, providing snippets of scenes. The two hollow youngsters can never be sure if it is all a charade or a dream, life or theatre. Is existence spontaneous improvisation from moment to moment? Or is there somewhere a master text with lines for us we have failed to study?❞
Alan Brien (Sunday Telegraph)

❝If the history of drama is chiefly the history of dramatists – and it is – then the National Theatre production of *Rosencrantz and Guildenstern are Dead* by Tom Stoppard is the most important event in the British professional theatre of the last nine years . . . Its ingenuity is stupendous; and the delicacy and complexity of its plot are handled with a theatrical mastery astonishing in a writer as young as Mr Stoppard, who, whilst demonstrating a spirit deep, foreboding, and compassionate like Beckett, shows a sleight of hand as cunning as Feydeau's.❞
Harold Hobson (Sunday Times)

Anthony Crickmay

All the plays that opened in 1967:

THE DANCE OF DEATH by August Strindberg, trans. by C. D. Locock, Dir. Glen Byam Shaw, Old Vic 21.2.67
ROSENCRANTZ AND GUILDENSTERN ARE DEAD by Tom Stoppard, Dir. Derek Goldby, Old Vic 11.4.67

THREE SISTERS by Anton Chekhov, trans. by Moura Budberg, Dir. Laurence Olivier, Old Vic 4.7.67
AS YOU LIKE IT by William Shakespeare, Dir. Clifford Williams, Old Vic 3.10.67

TARTUFFE by Molière, trans. by Richard Wilbur, Dir. Tyrone Guthrie, Old Vic 21.11.67

Zoë Dominic

John Gielgud (Oedipus), **Irene Worth** (Jocasta)

1968 OEDIPUS
by **Seneca**, adapted by
Ted Hughes from trans.
by **David Anthony Turner**

CAST: Alan Adams, Gillian Barge, David Belcher, Colin Blakely, Helen Bourne, Patrick Carter, Anna Carteret, Kenneth Colley, Oliver Cotton, Neil Fitzpatrick, Roger Forbes, Bernard Gallagher, John Gielgud, Jonathan Hardy, Luke Hardy, Roderick Horn, Gerald James, Lewis Jones, Richard Kay, Jane Lapotaire, Philip Locke, Harry Lomax, Kenneth Mackintosh, John Nightingale, Ronald Pickup, Louise Purnell, Jeremy Rowe, George Selway, Terence Taplin, Robert Tayman, Gary Waldhorn, Benjamin Whitrow, Judy Wilson, Peter Winter, Irene Worth, Frank Wylie.
Produced and designed by Peter Brook, *Associate producer* Geoffrey Reeves, *Music and sound organisation* Richard Peaslee, *Special costumes designed by* Jean Monod, *Lighting by* Robert Ornbo

❝At the end, with Jocasta self-impaled on Oedipus' sword and the blind king himself setting out to banishment, Mr Brook unexpectedly embarks on a wild anti-masque. The chorus puts on gaudy gold paper costumes and dances up and down the theater aisles and around an enormous golden phallic symbol to the accompaniment of a jazz band marching and playing "Yes We Have No Bananas!" The result is electrifying. The artificiality of the theater is flashed home with lightning speed . . . To say that this is a thrilling evening in the theater is to miss its purpose, because much more it is one of those rare evenings that force you to reassess what the theater is all about.❞
Clive Barnes (New York Times)

❝As Oedipus, John Gielgud, with all that iron control of his, pulls all the stops out and provides more anguished music than I have ever heard from him. He leaves us with a burning image of his mouth and eyes, reduced to three gaping holes.❞
Peter Lewis (Daily Mail)

All the plays that opened in 1968:

VOLPONE by Ben Jonson, Dir. Tyrone Guthrie, Old Vic 16.1.68
OEDIPUS by Seneca, adapted by Ted Hughes from trans. by David Anthony Turner, Dir. Peter Brook, Old Vic 19.3.68
EDWARD II by Bertolt Brecht, (after Christopher Marlowe), trans. by William E. Smith and Ralph Manheim, Dir. Frank Dunlop, Old Vic 30.4.68

TRIPLE BILL: *The Covent Garden Tragedy* by Henry Fielding, Dir. Robert Lang, *A Most Unwarrantable Intrusion* by John Maddison Morton, Dir. Robert Stephens, *In His Own Write* by John Lennon, Adrienne Kennedy, Victor Spinetti, Dir. Victor Spinetti, Old Vic 18.6.68

THE ADVERTISEMENT by Natalia Ginzburg, trans. by Henry Reed, Dir. Donald MacKechnie and Laurence Olivier, Old Vic 24.9.68
HOME AND BEAUTY by W. Somerset Maugham, Dir. Frank Dunlop, Old Vic 8.10.68
LOVE'S LABOUR'S LOST by William Shakespeare, Dir. Laurence Olivier, Old Vic 19.12.68

Above: **Robert Lang** (Ash), **Charles Kay** (Loach),
Brian Oulton (Mackie), **Isabelle Lucas** (Nurse Lake),
Bernard Gallagher (Foster), **Harry Lomax** (Flagg)

1969

THE NATIONAL HEALTH
by Peter Nichols

CAST: Gerald James *(Rees)*, Patrick Carter *(Tyler)*, Robert Lang *(Ash)*, Bernard Gallagher *(Foster)*, John Nightingale *(Ken)*, Harry Lomax *(Flagg)*, Charles Kay *(Loach)*, Brian Oulton *(Mackie)*, Mary Griffiths *(Matron)*, Maggie Riley *(Sister McPhee)*, Cleo Sylvestre *(Staff Nurse Norton)*, Anna Carteret *(Nurse Sweet)*, Isabelle Lucas *(Nurse Lake)*, Helen Fleming *(Nurse)*, Jim Dale *(Barnet)*, John Flint *(Michael)*, John Hamilton *(Prince)*, Paul Curran *(Mr Boyd)*, Robert Walker *(Neil)*, Gillian Barge *(Dr Bird)*, Malcolm Reid *(Indian student)*, Gabrielle Laye *(Old Woman)*, George Brown *(Chaplain)* Tom Baker, Frederick Bennett, Jean Boht, Michael Edgar, Roger Forbes, Michael Harding, Norma Streader *(Theatre staff, visitors, etc)*
Musicians: Jack Botterell, Laurie Morgan, Norman Wells, Rod Wilmott
Production by Michael Blakemore, *Designed by* Patrick Robertson, *Lighting by* Robert Bryan, *Music by* Marc Wilkinson, *Movement by* Claude Chagrin, *Cakewalk by* Malcolm Goddard

❝I find the humour of life a great reward for its discomforts. It is not necessarily an escape, but part of the fabric of life. I think hospitals are hilarious as well as sad. I was in four hospitals with a collapsed lung. I also met my wife there.❞
Peter Nichols

❝On one level it is a sort of Carry On National Health Service, complete with bedpan jokes and busty nurses and highly comic, desperately ill patients. On another it is a brilliantly ruthless and stingingly funny examination of a situation where people are, on the one hand, not allowed to die, and on the other not helped much to live. I was not the only one who laughed myself nearly sick enough to require treatment at the nearest out-patients.❞
Ann Pacey (The Sun)

❝Peter Nichols comes smilingly towards us in the green gloom of a hospital ward, anaesthetising us with laughter in order to apply the knife to our taboos. His real subject is the fear of pain and death, which society and the National Health does not allow the patients to mention, covering it up with hypocritical cheerfulness, and wonder medicine that pulls back people from the doors of a timely death.❞
Peter Lewis (Daily Mail)

All the plays that opened in 1969:

'H' by Charles Wood, Dir. Geoffrey Reeves, Old Vic 13.2.69
THE WAY OF THE WORLD by William Congreve, Dir. Michael Langham, Old Vic 1.5.69

MACRUNE'S GUEVARA by John Spurling, Dir. Frank Dunlop and Robert Stephens, and RITES by Maureen Duffy, Dir. Joan Plowright, Old Vic 27.5.69
BACK TO METHUSELAH by Bernard Shaw, Dir. Clifford Williams with Donald MacKechnie, Old Vic, *Part I* 31.7.69, *Part II* 1.8.69

THE NATIONAL HEALTH by Peter Nichols, Dir. Michael Blakemore, Old Vic 16.10.69
THE WHITE DEVIL by John Webster, Dir. Frank Dunlop, Old Vic 13.11.69
THE TRAVAILS OF SANCHO PANZA by James Saunders, Dir. Donald MacKechnie and Joan Plowright, Old Vic 18.12.69

❛I had my new teeth [specially made for the part] and immediately I felt right. My only concern was that Jonathan Miller might take one look and confiscate them. But I think he was so relieved that I hadn't put on a false nose, he willingly let me keep them.❜
Laurence Olivier (On Acting)

❛At the beginning there was a real danger of Olivier shaping a too grotesque caricature, a full-blown hook nose and all the rest. You can only go so far in seeking to restrain an actor of such stature and individual technique.❜
Jonathan Miller

❛No one will forget this Shylock's infernal dance of triumph, oddly reminiscent of Hitler at the Arc-de-Triomphe, when he learns that Antonio's argosy is wrecked, or his kneeling, broken to weep at the loss of the turquoise his daughter had stolen.❜
John Barber (Daily Telegraph)

❛I find it impossible to think of Shylock as a really nice chap; he is just better quality stuff than any of the Christians in the play. They are truly vile, heartless, money-grubbing monsters and when Shylock makes his final exit, destroyed by defeat, one should sense that our Christian brothers are at last thoroughly ashamed of themselves.❜
Laurence Olivier (Confessions of an Actor)

Below: **Joan Plowright** (Portia), **Jeremy Brett** (Bassanio), **Benjamin Whitrow** (Duke of Venice), **Laurence Olivier** (Shylock), **Derek Jacobi** (Gratiano)

1970

THE MERCHANT OF VENICE
by William Shakespeare

CAST: Benjamin Whitrow *(Duke of Venice),* Tom Baker *(Prince of Morocco),* Charles Kay *(Prince of Arragon),* Anthony Nicholls *(Antonio),* Jeremy Brett *(Bassanio),* Michael Tudor Barnes *(Solanio),* Derek Jacobi *(Gratiano),* Richard Kay *(Salerio),* Malcolm Reid *(Lorenzo),* Laurence Olivier *(Shylock),* Lewis Jones *(Tubal),* Jim Dale *(Launcelot Gobbo),* Harry Lomax *(Old Gobbo),* Lawrence Trimble *(Servant to Antonio),* Alan Dudley *(Leonardo),* Michael Harding *(Balthasar),* Patrick Carter *(Stephano),* Joan Plowright *(Portia),* Anna Carteret *(Nerissa),* Gillian Barge *(Servant to Portia),* Jane Lapotaire *(Jessica),* Laura Sarti, Clare Walmesley *(Singers)*
Hugh Armstrong, Kate Coleridge, Michael Edgar, Sean Roantree, Lawrence Trimble, Paul Vousden *(Officers, servants,etc)*
Musicians: Benedict Cruft, Chuck Mallet, Nigel Pinkett
Production by Jonathan Miller, *Designed by* Julia Trevelyan Oman, *Lighting by* Robert Ornbo, *Musical arrangements and original music by* Carl Davis

Anthony Crickmay

Zoë Dominic

Above: **Maggie Smith** (Hedda)

CAST: Jeremy Brett *(George Tesman)*, Maggie Smith *(Hedda Tesman)*, Jeanne Watts *(Juliana Tesman)*, Sheila Reid *(Mrs Elvsted)*, John Moffatt *(Judge Brack)*, Robert Stephens *(Eilert Loevborg)*, Julia McCarthy *(Bertha)*
Production by Ingmar Bergman, *Designed by* Mago

1970

HEDDA GABLER
by **Henrik Ibsen**,
trans. by **Michael Meyer**

❛The whole thing is like a casket for some precious stone, in this case the priceless and wonderful Hedda of Maggie Smith. Through a daring innovation of the director's she opens the play, wandering on in a white nightdress, pallid and fraught, a picture of silent agony; she studies herself in the full-length looking-glass – her narcissism is a great feature of this Hedda – and passes her hands over her body with a rictus of disgust as she contemplates the fact of her pregnancy.❜
Anthony Curtis (Financial Times)

❛A bare red cage of imprisoned passion: a windowless chamber in the skull of General Gabler's daughter where she dreams the sex, power and violence she dare not act in life. The Chinese box set Ibsen prescribed has been turned inside out. The inner sanctum to which Hedda retires to brood and punish her piano, from which she emerges like a tigress raiding sheep, has been brought forward to share half the stage. Throughout the play, she's visible in it, listening behind the sliding doors to her husband and guests, pacing and snarling to herself at their genteel inanities, fondling the pistols her father left her.❜
Ronald Bryden (Observer)

Reg Wilson

1971 THE CAPTAIN OF KÖPENICK
by Carl Zuckmayer, adapted by John Mortimer

CAST: Jim Dale *(Kalle)*, Andrew Dowling *(Billiards Attendant/Convict)*, Peter Duncan *(Helmut)*, John Flint *(Bulcke/Soldier)*, Bill Fraser *(Obermüller)*, Bernard Gallagher *(Sergeant/Hoprecht/Inspector)*, Mary Griffiths *(Frau Hoprecht)*, Michael Harding *(Waiter/Convict/Kutzmann)*, Edward Hardwicke *(Buttje/Capt. von Schleinitz/Passport Official)*, James Hayes *(Höllhuber/Convict/Lieutenant/Officer/Soldier)*, David Henry *(Zeck/Convict/Corporal)*, Stephen Howe *(Child)*, Hazel Hughes *(Frau Obermüller)*, Gerald James *(Policeman/Governor/Porter)*, Brian Jameson *(Convict/Soldier)*, Lewis Jones *(Corporal/Convict/Soldier/Policeman/Commissioner/Photographer)*, Charles Kay *(Superintendent/General)*, Richard Kay *(Willy Wormser/Soldier/Stutz)*, David Kincaid *(Grenadier/Warder/Soldier)*, Jane Lapotaire *(Lieschen/Old Lady)*, Gabrielle Laye *(Tart/Augusta)*, Denis Lill *(Gebweiler/Convict/Officer/Soldier)*, Harry Lomax *(Wabschke/Veteran/Councillor)*, Julia McCarthy *(Fanny/Old Lady/Peasant Girl)*, Richard McCormick *(Child)*, Kenneth Mackintosh *(Wormser/Superintendent)*, John Moffatt *(Von Schlettow/Krakauer/Chief of Police)*, Ronald Pickup *(Dr Jellinek/Field Marshal/Rosencrantz)*, Malcolm Reid *(Deltzeit/Convict/Soldier/Police Inspector)*, Maggie Riley *(Polly/Nurse)*, David Ryall *(Sergeant/Convict/Kilian)*, Paul Scofield *(Wilhelm Voigt)*, Stephen Sheppard *(Trump/Soldier/Policeman)*, Norma Streader *(Nurse/Sarah)*, Brian Tully *(Chaplain/Kessler/Councillor)*, Michael Turner *(Dosshouse keeper/Police Inspector)*, Jane Wenham *(Tart/Frau Kessler)*, Derek Woodward *(Jupp/Convict/Soldier)*
Musicians: Sebastian Bell, Jack Botterall, Martin Fry, Michael Harris, Michael Laird, Michael Lankester, Laurie Morgan, Norman Wells
Production by Frank Dunlop, *Design by* Karl von Appen, *Lighting by* John B Read, *Music by* Michael Lankester, *Dances by* Sheila O'Neill

❝John Mortimer's adaptation divides the play almost equally between the biography of William Voigt, the historical imposter condemned to an unpersoned life of jails, doss-houses and deportations by lack of an official pass, and that of the uniform he hires to steal one from Köpenick town hall. In a boisterous new party-scene it's worn by the maker's daughter and sexually excites both men and women alike. Its symbolic menace is underlined in a Carlylean speech about clothes, civilizations and appearances. "Even this great stone Berlin of ours" muses Voigt, "does it not stand on sand, shifting sand?" The silhouette of the waste-land Hitler made of it falls for a moment across the play.❞
Ronald Bryden (Observer)

❝Listen to the sudden, naked, painfully intimate "please" with which he embarrasses what must be his millionth negative bureaucrat; watch him slump back momentarily into his old dazed, defeated self as his captives tell him they don't keep passports at Köpenick. The eyelids drop, the shoulders slightly sag, the mouth opens a little, and it is done. No one who values the art of acting should miss this performance.❞
Benedict Nightingale (New Statesman)

❝Voigt has been played by the greatest German actors, but Scofield is one of the best I have ever seen. Such understanding, such distinction.❞
Carl Zuckmayer

Zoë Dominic

Laurence Olivier (James Tyrone), **Constance Cummings** (Mary Cavan Tyrone), **Denis Quilley** (Jamie), **Ronald Pickup** (Edmund)

1971

LONG DAY'S JOURNEY INTO NIGHT
by Eugene O'Neill

CAST: Laurence Olivier *(James Tyrone)*, Constance Cummings *(Mary Cavan Tyrone)*, Denis Quilley *(Jamie)*, Ronald Pickup *(Edmund)*, Maureen Lipman *(Cathleen)*
Production by Michael Blakemore, *Designs by* Michael Annals, *Lighting by* Robert Bryan

❝In one day O'Neill shows us how this family crumbles under the weight of its jealousies, its hatreds, its recriminations. The mother returns to drugs after there seemed to be some hope for a cure. The youngest son is told he has TB and the father is ready to send him to a cheap sanatorium to save money. The curtain falls on the three males in the family – drunk, silent and beaten – listening to the drug-sodden mother eerily recalling the fragmentary moments in her life when she was happy. It is a shattering theatrical moment which reaches deep down into the the troubled and agonised psyche of any audience.❞
Milton Shulman (Evening Standard)

❝The part of Tyrone is one of the richest ever written: very long but nearly perfect. The repetition's a challenge, a delicious little problem to overcome, but then I enjoy challenges.❞
Laurence Olivier (On Acting)

❝What marks out this performance most from the others is its breadth; all the components of the man are there simultaneously – the tight-wad, the old pro, the distracted husband, the ragged Irish boy – and there is the sense not only that O'Neill is showing off the different sides of the character, but that Olivier is consciously manipulating them for his advantage.❞
Irving Wardle (The Times)

TYGER by Adrian Mitchell with music by Mike Westbrook, Dir. Michael Blakemore and John Dexter, New Theatre 20.7.71
DANTON'S DEATH by George Buchner, adapted by John Wells, Dir. Jonathan Miller, New Theatre 3.8.71

THE GOOD NATURED MAN by Oliver Goldsmith, Dir. John Dexter, Old Vic 9.12.71
LONG DAY'S JOURNEY INTO NIGHT by Eugene O'Neill, Dir. Michael Blakemore, New Theatre 21.12.71

1972 JUMPERS
by Tom Stoppard

❝On a vast white bed Diana Rigg lies half-naked, playing a ravishing pop-singer who has lately collapsed at a public appearance and is now in the care of a demonic psychiatrist. Michael Hordern, as her husband, a philosophy professor, is next door, dictating an endless lecture on whether God exists.❞
John Barber (Daily Telegraph)

Peter Wood: When I first asked you what the play was about, you said "It's about a man trying to write a lecture". But for me it was about a man trying to write a lecture *while his wife was stuck with a corpse in the next room.*

Tom Stoppard: I have to confess that the *plot*, the story, comes so far behind the initial impetus for the play, that in this case I didn't even know who the corpse was or who had shot him or why. That was a little problem I would settle in due course. Not that the origin of the play was exclusively intellectual. Simultaneously I fell for the image of a pyramid of gymnasts occupying the stage, followed by a gunshot, followed by the image of one gymnast being shot out of the pyramid and the others imploding on the hole.
(from the programme for the NT's revival in 1976)

CAST: Anna Carteret *(Secretary),* Paul Curran *(Crouch),* Diana Rigg *(Dottie),* Michael Hordern *(George),* David Ryall *(Bones),* Graham Crowden *(Archie),* Desmond McNamara *(Scott),* Allan Mitchell *(Greystoke),* David Howey *(Clegthorpe),* Ray Callaghan, Tom Dickinson, Michael Edgar, Tom Georgeson, Lionel Guyett, William Hobbs, David Howey, Barry James, Brian Jameson, Desmond McNamara, Riggs O'Hara, Howard Southern, Harry Waters *(Jumpers),* Ray Callaghan, Tom Georgeson, Lionel Guyett, James Hayes, Barry James, Maureen Lipman, Riggs O'Hara, Howard Southern *(Ushers, tourists, etc)*
Musicians: Chuck Mallet, Laurie Morgan, Mike Page
Production by Peter Wood, *Settings by* Patrick Robertson, *Costumes by* Rosemary Vercoe, *Lighting by* Robert Bryan, *Original music by* Marc Wilkinson, *Original lyrics by* Tom Stoppard, *Choreography by* Malcolm Goddard

Michael Hordern (George)

Zoë Dominic

Diana Rigg (Dottie)

All the plays that opened in 1972:

JUMPERS by Tom Stoppard, Dir. Peter Wood, Old Vic 2.2.72
RICHARD II by William Shakespeare, Dir. David William, Old Vic 29.3.72

THE SCHOOL FOR SCANDAL by Richard Brinsley Sheridan, Dir. Jonathan Miller, Old Vic 11.5.72
THE FRONT PAGE by Ben Hecht and Charles MacArthur, Dir. Michael Blakemore, Old Vic 6.7.72

'TIS PITY SHE'S A WHORE by John Ford, Dir. Roland Joffe, Old Vic 18.7.72 (Mobile)
MACBETH by William Shakespeare, Dir. Michael Blakemore, Old Vic 9.11.72

Sophie Baker

Above: **Denis Quilley** (Hildy Johnson),
Alan MacNaughtan (Walter Burns)

1972 THE FRONT PAGE
by **Ben Hecht** and **Charles MacArthur**

CAST: Allan Mitchell *(Wilson)*, John Shrapnel *(Endicott)*, James Hayes *(Murphy)*, Gawn Grainger *(McCue)*, David Bradley *(Schwartz)*, David Ryall *(Kruger)*, Benjamin Whitrow *(Bensinger)*, Maggie Riley *(Mrs Schlosser)*, David Henry *(Woodenshoes Eichhorn)*, Stephen Greif *(Diamond Louie)*, Denis Quilley *(Hildy Johnson)*, Jeanne Watts *(Jennie)*, Maureen Lipman *(Mollie Malloy)*, David Bauer *(Sheriff Hartman)*, Anna Carteret *(Peggy Grant)*, Mary Griffiths *(Mrs Grant)*, Paul Curran *(The Mayor)*, Harry Lomax *(Mr Pincus)*, Clive Merrison *(Earl Williams)*, Alan MacNaughtan *(Walter Burns)*, Barry James *(Tony)*, Kenneth Mackintosh *(Carl)*, Malcolm Reid *(Frank)*, Michael Essex, Paul Hetherington, David Kincaid, Roger Monk, Harry Waters, David Whitman *(Policemen etc)*
Production by Michael Blakemore, *Design by* Michael Annals, *Lighting by* Leonard Tucker

❛"Who the hell's going to read the second paragraph?" snarls the cynical, check-suited newspaper editor in Ben Hecht and Charles MacArthur's *The Front Page*. So, just in case, let me say at once that the National Theatre revival of this racy, witty, exuberant 1928 Broadway comedy is a cracking example of the entertainment theatre at its best.❜
Michael Billington (Guardian)

❛It is one of the very few plays in which we are shown people actually earning their living, and the first act in particular has the fascination of a building site. We see the restless ethnic mix of America pushing towards that extra buck that promises security and peace of mind.❜
Michael Blakemore (from the programme for the Australian tour, 1973)

❛The telephones bring eagerly awaited non-stop messages of the atrocious, ghoulish and obscene activities that will fill the columns and boost circulation. The last is the sole moral criterion . . . The more powerful figures are also the most corrupt. Graft is the accepted currency. With an election pending the Mayor has recourse to the Red Menace and worries about the black vote. The enormity of their dishonesty is positively relished by the authors. Ironically, it is this morally dubious lack of indignation which ensures the play's success as a farce.❜
Frank Marcus (Sunday Telegraph)

Zoe Dominic

1973/4 THE MISANTHROPE
by Molière, Eng. version by Tony Harrison

CAST: Alec McCowen *(Alceste)*, Alan MacNaughtan *(Philinte)*, Gawn Grainger *(Oronte)*, Diana Rigg *(Célimène)*, Jeanne Watts *(Eliante)*, Gillian Barge *(Arsinoé)*, Nicholas Clay *(Acaste)*, Jeremy Clyde *(Clitandre)*, Paul Curran *(Basque)*, Clive Merrison *(Official of the Académie Française)*, James Hayes *(Dubois)*
Production by John Dexter, *Design by* Tanya Moiseiwitsch, *Lighting by* Andy Phillips, *Music arranged by* Marc Wilkinson

❛What a marvellous idea to turn Molière's satire on the Sun King's artificial society into a lampoon on the conceits as practised in the reign of that other absolute French monarch, Charles de Gaulle. Of course we preened ourselves that the Sixties was an era of new social honesty and revolution. But Tony Harrison's audacious, updated translation proves otherwise. The characters created some 300 years ago swan their way effortlessly and elegantly into the pools of our own recent past.❜
Jack Tinker (Daily Mail)

❛In Alceste (Mr McCowen) the Misanthropic hero, Molière drew the ultimate portrait of a man of sincerity trying to maintain standards of truth in a heartless, superficial society. His ideals come to grief and he is made to grovel because of his hopeless infatuation for the utterly fickle Celimene (Miss Rigg). Though striking moral attitudes, Mr McCowen doesn't seem a prig. He never loses sympathy because his Alceste always retains a quality of critical – almost amused – self-appraisal. Here is a performance of astonishing variety of pace and tone. As for Miss Rigg – radiating fatal femininity in revealing dresses – she completely fulfils Alceste's description of "a baited barb of beauty".❜
Felix Barker (Evening News)

Diana Rigg (Celimene), **Alec McCowen** (Alceste)

All the plays that opened in 1973:

TWELFTH NIGHT by William Shakespeare, Dir. Peter James, Old Vic 4.1.73 (Mobile)
THE MISANTHROPE by Molière, English version by Tony Harrison, Dir. John Dexter, Old Vic 22.2.73

THE CHERRY ORCHARD by Anton Chekhov, Dir. Michael Blakemore, Old Vic 24.5.73
EQUUS by Peter Shaffer, Dir. John Dexter, Old Vic 26.7.73
THE BACCHAE by Euripides, adapted by Wole Soyinka, Dir. Roland Joffé, Old Vic 2.8.73

SATURDAY SUNDAY MONDAY
by Eduardo de Filippo, trans. by Keith Waterhouse and Willis Hall, Dir. Franco Zeffirelli, Old Vic 25.10.73
THE PARTY by Trevor Griffiths, Dir. John Dexter, Old Vic 20.12.73

1973/4

EQUUS
by Peter Shaffer

CAST: Alec McCowen *(Martin Dysart),* Louie Ramsay *(Nurse),* Gillian Barge *(Hesther Saloman),* Peter Firth *(Alan Strang),* Alan MacNaughtan *(Frank Strang),* Jeanne Watts *(Dora Strang),* Nicholas Clay *(Horseman),* David Healy *(Harry Dalton),* Doran Godwin *(Jill Mason),* Keith Skinner *(Derek Dalton) with* Neil Cunningham, David Graham, David Kincaid, Maggie Riley, Rosalind Shanks, Veronica Sowerby, Harry Waters
Production by John Dexter, *Designs by* John Napier, *Music by* Marc Wilkinson, *Lighting by* Andy Phillips, *Movement by* Claude Chagrin

❝One weekend over two years ago I was driving with a friend through bleak country-side. We passed a stable. Suddenly he was reminded by it of an alarming crime [a boy blinding horses] which he had heard about recently at a dinner party in London. He knew only one horrible detail, and his complete mention of it could barely have lasted a minute – but it was enough to arouse in me an intense fascination.❞
Peter Shaffer (NT's programme)

❝The scene is like a boxing ring or bull-fight arena, with the audience ranged on two sides. It represents the room of a psychiatrist, terrifyingly bare, a room professionally dedicated to the driving out of devils from the minds of patients so that – this is Mr Shaffer's frightening thesis – other devils may enter worse than those that have been expelled.❞
Harold Hobson (Sunday Times)

❝The theatrical impact of *Equus* is breathtaking. John Dexter's clean-limbed production goes as far as it can in enhancing the play's equestrian imagery while the acting by the two leading players is superb . . . Quite simply, *Equus* is magnificent.❞
Clive Hirschhorn (Sunday Express)

John Haynes

Above: **Peter Firth** (Alan Strang), **Nicholas Clay** (Horseman)

All the plays that opened in 1974:

MEASURE FOR MEASURE by William Shakespeare, Dir. Jonathan Miller, Old Vic 15.1.74 (Mobile)
THE TEMPEST by William Shakespeare, Dir. Peter Hall, Old Vic 5.3.74

EDEN END by J. B. Priestley, Dir. Laurence Olivier, Old Vic 4.4.74
NEXT OF KIN by John Hopkins, Dir. Harold Pinter, Old Vic 2.5.74

SPRING AWAKENING by Frank Wedekind, trans. by Edward Bond, Dir. Bill Bryden, Old Vic 28.5.74
THE MARRIAGE OF FIGARO by Beaumarchais, trans. by John Wells, Dir. Jonathan Miller, Old Vic 9.7.74

❝De Filippo moves his characters with such absolute understanding of humanity in general, and of theirs in particular, that he manages to restate some abiding truths in a way which ensures that our belief in them is permanently reinforced. He hides none of the bars that surround the cage in which his family lives, in which so many families live; he does not even wrap the bars in coloured paper. But he shows that the tensions of family life are inseparable from its strength and values, and it is that residual strength and those eternal values that his play celebrates.❞ *Bernard Levin (The Times)*

❝For all their zip, the Priores cast shadows. Grandpa gets a big laugh from the family and the audience when he wonders out loud how many more Sundays he'll be on earth to take such abuse. But you can imagine him alone at night asking himself the same question. Papa's hang-dog jealousy is funny, but when he tells Mama that he almost shot her supposed lover at dinner, we can see how easily the play could have gone another way without really shifting gears. The laughs here are the kind that can die in the throat.❞
Dan Sullivan (Los Angeles Times)

❝This is the best-smelling show in town. Real food is served on stage. Oh, those mouth-watering odours!❞
Arthur Thirkell (Daily Mirror)

Background: **Desmond McNamara** (Michele), **Martin Shaw** (Attilio), **Laurence Olivier** (Antonio), **Anna Carteret** (Virginia), **David Healy** (Rafaele); *At table, clockwise from left:* **Frank Finlay** (Peppino), **Maggie Riley** (Maria), **Denis Quilley** (Luigi Ianniello), **Joan** **Plowright** (Rosa), **David Graham** (Dr Cefercola), **Mary Griffiths** (Aunt Meme), **Nicholas Clay** (Rocco), **Clive Merrison** (Federico), **Jeanne Watts** (Elena), **Gawn Grainger** (Roberto), **Louise Purnell** (Guilianella)

47

1973/4

SATURDAY SUNDAY MONDAY
by Eduardo de Filippo,
trans. by **Keith Waterhouse**
and **Willis Hall**

CAST: Laurence Olivier *(Antonio)*, Joan Plowright *(Rosa)*, Frank Finlay *(Peppino)*, Mary Griffiths *(Aunt Meme)*, Martin Shaw *(Attilio)*, David Healy *(Raffaele)*, Gawn Grainger *(Roberto)*, Nicholas Clay *(Rocco)*, Louise Purnell *(Guilianella)*, Clive Merrison *(Federico)*, Maggie Riley *(Maria)*, Denis Quilley *(Luigi Ianniello)*, Jeanne Watts *(Elena)*, Anna Carteret *(Virginia)*, Desmond McNamara *(Michele)*, Harry Lomax *(Catiello)*, David Graham *(Dr Cefercola)*
Musicians: Bobby Campbell, Henry Krein, John Trusler
Directed by Franco Zeffirelli, *Scenery by* Franco Zeffirelli, *Costumes by* Raimonda Gaetani, *Lighting by* Leonard Tucker, *Musical arrangements by* Michael Lankester

Zoë Dominic

ROMEO AND JULIET by William Shakespeare,
Dir. Bill Bryden, Old Vic 13.9.74 (Mobile)
THE FREEWAY by Peter Nichols, Dir. Jonathan Miller,
Old Vic 1.10.74
GRAND MANOEUVRES by A. E. Ellis,
Dir. Michael Blakemore, Old Vic 3.12.74

1975

JOHN GABRIEL BORKMAN
by Henrik Ibsen, trans. by Inga-Stina Ewbank and Peter Hall

CAST: Wendy Hiller *(Gunhild Borkman),* Barbara Keogh *(Maid),* Peggy Ashcroft *(Ella Rentheim),* Frank Grimes *(Erhart Borkman),* Anna Carteret *(Fanny Wilton),* Ralph Richardson *(John Gabriel Borkman),* Cheryl Campbell *(Frida Foldal),* Alan Webb *(William Foldal)*

Directed by Peter Hall, *Settings and costumes by* Timothy O'Brien and Tazeena Firth, *Assistant to the designers* Robert Harris, *Lighting by* David Hersey

Zoë Dominic

Frank Grimes (Erhart Borkman), **Wendy Hiller** (Gunhild Borkman), **Peggy Ashcroft** (Ella Rentheim), **Ralph Richardson** (John Gabriel Borkman)

❝I've got the John, I've got the Borkman, I'm still looking for the Gabriel.❞
Ralph Richardson in rehearsal

❝There are moments in this performance when Borkman speaks utterly prosaic words in a manner entirely normal, and yet it is evident that the man is completely and frighteningly mad. There is something both wholly natural, given Borkman's character, and strangely disturbing in the Napoleonic gesture of hand-stuck-into-the-shirt-front when he receives a visitor.❞
Harold Hobson (Sunday Times)

❝I shall never forget the noise he made when Borkman died. As if a bird had flown out of his heart.❞
John Gielgud

❝It is a perilous trek, but Peter Hall's production makes the ascent with miraculous sure-footedness. Reaching the heights of all Ibsen's greatness, it encompasses the contradictions of the text with something like a lover's embrace. A bleak humour is shot through the evening which touches the deepest ironies in the human heart. Wendy Hiller, having swooped on every trait that life as Borkman's wife has fed her, fairly licks her lips in pleased smiles as she tastes the long-dried blood. By contrast Dame Peggy Ashcroft gives her adversary, sister Ella, the softness of embalmed goodness.❞
Jack Tinker (Daily Mail)

All the plays that opened in 1975:

JOHN GABRIEL BORKMAN by Henrik Ibsen, trans. by Inga-Stina Ewbank and Peter Hall, Dir. Peter Hall, Old Vic 28.1.75
HEARTBREAK HOUSE by Bernard Shaw, Dir. John Schlesinger, Old Vic 25.2.75

HAPPY DAYS by Samuel Beckett, Dir. Peter Hall, Old Vic 13.3.75
NO MAN'S LAND by Harold Pinter, Dir. Peter Hall, Old Vic 23.4.75
ENGAGED by W. S. Gilbert, Dir. Michael Blakemore, Old Vic 6.8.75

PHAEDRA BRITANNICA by Tony Harrison after Racine, Dir. John Dexter, Old Vic 9.9.75
PLAYBOY OF THE WESTERN WORLD by J. M. Synge, Dir. Bill Bryden, Old Vic 29.10.75

1975

NO MAN'S LAND
by Harold Pinter

CAST: Ralph Richardson *(Hirst)*, John Gielgud *(Spooner)*, Michael Feast *(Foster)*, Terence Rigby *(Briggs)*
Directed by Peter Hall, *Designed by* John Bury, *Assistant to the Designer* Timian Alsaker

Anthony Crickmay

Left: **Ralph Richardson** (Hirst),
John Gielgud (Spooner)

❝At our first night party afterwards John said to Harold that playing Pinter was like playing Congreve or Wilde. It needed a consciousness of the audience, a manipulation of them which was precisely the same as for high classical comedy. He thought it would be like playing Chekhov – where you must ignore the audience – but it wasn't. He's damned right.❞
Peter Hall (Peter Hall's Diaries)

❝Harold Pinter's new play, *No Man's Land*, is about precisely what its title suggests: the sense of being caught in some mysterious limbo between life and death, between a world of brute reality and one of fluid uncertainty. But although plenty of plays have tried to pin down that strange sense of reaching out into a void, I can think of few that have done so as concretely, funnily and concisely as Pinter's.❞
Michael Billington (The Guardian)

❝John's performance is magnificent, but there are other actors who could do it, whereas I do not think any other actor could fill Hirst with such a sense of loneliness and creativity as Ralph does.❞
Peter Hall (Peter Hall's Diaries)

❝The precision, understanding and ear for musical nuances of Peter Hall's direction are masterly. It is a miraculous evening of aesthetic pleasure, strictly unsuitable for the unimaginative.❞
Frank Marcus (Sunday Telegraph)

HAMLET by William Shakespeare, Dir. Peter Hall, Old Vic 10.12.75
JUDGEMENT by Barry Collins, Dir. Peter Hall, Old Vic 18.12.75

John Haynes

Susan Fleetwood (Pegeen Mike),
Stephen Rea (Christy Mahon)

1975

PLAYBOY OF THE WESTERN WORLD
by J. M. Synge

CAST: Stephen Rea *(Christopher Mahon)*, J G Devlin *(Old Mahon)*, Liam Redmond *(Michael James Flaherty)*, Susan Fleetwood *(Margaret Flaherty (Pegeen Mike))*, Jim Norton *(Sean Keogh)*, P G Stephens *(Philly O'Cullen)*, Eddie Byrne *(Jimmy Farrell)*, Margaret Whiting *(Widow Quin)*, Jeananne Crowley *(Sara Tansey)*, Rynagh O'Grady *(Susan Brady)*, Nora Connolly *(Honor Blake)*, Terry Donnelly *(Nelly McLaughlin)*, Harry Webster *(Bellman)*, Pitt Wilkinson, Michael Keating *(Peasants)*
Musicians: Bobby Casey, Marion McCarthy, Tommy McCarthy, Laurie Morgan
Directed by Bill Bryden, *Settings by* Geoffrey Scott, *Costumes by* Deirdre Clancy, *Lighting by* Leonard Tucker, *Music by* The Chieftains

❝Anyone who has lived in real intimacy with the Irish peasantry will know that the wildest sayings and ideas in this play are tame indeed, compared with the fancies one may hear in any little hillside cabin in Geesala, or Carraroe, or Dingle Bay.❞
J. M. Synge

❝There are nights when the stage breaks its banks, unleashing a torrent of passion and joy. Such it was for me last night as Bill Bryden's production of Synge's intoxicating play now held us in rapt silence, now caused us to laugh with our guts.❞
Charles Lewsen (The Times)

❝Why did I want to weep at the exultant moment of Christy's greatest triumph, when he is carried in by the village people after winning all the major events at the sports and presented with his prizes? It was not at his subsequent humiliation that I had the urge, nor when all his easily won victories are torn from him and replaced by shame, nor at the moment of Pegeen Mike's realisation that the victorious figure she had set her mind on had been brought to dust. It was at the cheers of the villagers for their new hero, the boy who had killed his father with one blow of his spade. It is all too relevant to what goes on today.❞
B. A. Young (Financial Times)

'Champagne, the Charleston, the posse of servants, the lint-white cleanliness of the jokes – all are vintage 1928. "You'll have to go a long way to get round *me*" snarls the large bad-tempered lady. "I'd have to take a taxi" says the dude.'
John Barber (Daily Telegraph)

'With a little adjustment and a little more violence, *Plunder* would soon cease to be a laughing matter; which, I think, is its real claim to the classic rank. Great farce always is a precarious experience, in which comedy barely escapes being engulfed by horror and disaster . . . To pick one example, here's D'Arcy in the bedroom hovering over the sleeping Mrs Hewlett with a phial of knock-out drops while Malone is rifling her jewel case. Experimentally he uncorks it and has a sniff, and knocks himself out. The effect is hilarious, but you suppress your laughter for fear of awakening the sleeping dragon.'
Irving Wardle (The Times)

'Mr Landen has a uniquely fussy mode of locomotion which would ensure him swift promotion in the Ministry of Funny Walks; and he can fall like a stricken oak.'
Harold Hobson (Sunday Times)

Below: **Frank Finlay** (Freddy Malone), **Dandy Nichols** (Mrs Hewlett), **Peter Rocca** (Plain Clothes Detective), **Glyn Grain** (Det. Sgt. Marchant), **Derek Newark** (Det. Insp. Sibley), **Dinsdale Landen** (D'Arcy Tuck)

1976
PLUNDER
by Ben Travers

CAST: Trevor Ray *(Oswald Veal),* Diana Quick *(Prudence Malone),* Dandy Nichols *(Mrs Hewlett),* Paul Dawkins *(Simon Veal),* Frank Finlay *(Freddy Malone),* Catherine Harding *(Mabel),* Polly Adams *(Joan Hewlett),* Dinsdale Landen *(D'Arcy Tuck),* Michael Beint *(Sir George Chudleigh),* Brenda Kaye *(Lady Chudleigh),* Michael Keating *(Harry Kenward),* Carol Frazer *(Ruth Bennett),* Ray Edwards *(Footman),* Desmond Adams *(William),* Michael Stroud *(Buckley),* Barbara Keogh *(Mrs Orlock),* Daniel Thorndike *(Chief Constable Grierson),* Derek Newark *(Detective Inspector Sibley),* Andrew Hilton *(Police Constable Davis),* Glyn Grain *(Detective Sergeant Marchant),* Patrick Monckton *(Detective Sergeant Bryant),* Peter Rocca *(Plain Clothes Detective),* Rose Power *(Cook),* Brenda Blethyn, Nora Connolly, Jeananne Crowley, Rynagh O'Grady *(Maids)*
Directed by Michael Blakemore, *Designed by* Michael Annals, *Lighting by* Leonard Tucker

Zoë Dominic

Right: **Barbara Jefford** (Zabina),
Denis Quilley (Bajazeth), **Albert
Finney** (Tamburlaine)

Nobby Clark

CAST: Desmond Adams (Soldier/First Messenger), Jonathan Battersby (Soldier), Michael Beint (Menaphon/King of Trebizon), Brenda Blethyn (Ebea), Timothy Block (Messenger), Norman Claridge (King of Fez/Frederick/First Citizen), Oliver Cotton (Techelles), Brian Cox (Theridamas), Jeananne Crowley (First Virgin), Robert Eddison (Prologue/Orcanes), Ray Edwards (Soldier), Albert Finney (Tamburlaine), Susan Fleetwood (Zenocrate), Carol Frazer (Second Virgin), Angela Galbraith (Anippe), John Gill (Basso/Governor of Babylon), Michael Gough (Soldan of Egypt), Glyn Grain (Soldier/Attendant/King of Amasia), Gawn Grainger (Usumcasane), Andrew Hilton (King of Arabia/Second Citizen), Barbara Jefford (Zabina), Michael Keating (Capolin/Third Messenger), Brian Kent (King of Jerusalem), Robin Keston (Olympia's son), Stanley Lloyd (Soldier), Philip Locke (Mycetes), Harry Lomax (Ceneus/Gazellus), Kenneth Mackintosh (Ortygius), Mark McManus (Amyras), Michael Melia (King of Argier/Captain of Balsera), Patrick Monckton (Perdicas), Virginia Moore (Attendant), Jeffrey Morgan (Soldier), Peter Needham (Spy/Governor of Damascus/Uribassa/Maximus), John Nettleton (Agydas/Sigismund), Derek Newark (Almeda), Jim Norton (Calyphas), Liam O'Callaghan (Soldier), Diana Quick (Olympia), Denis Quilley (Bajazeth/Callapine), Catherine Riding (Attendant), Ray Roberts (Second Messenger), Peter Rocca (Messenger), Struan Rodger (Celebinus), Gerard Salih (Olympia's son), Nicholas Selby (Meander/Physician), Sarah Simmons (Attendant), Philip Stone (Cosroe), Daniel Thorndike (King of Morocco/Baldwin/King of Soria), Dennis Tynsley (Soldier), Harry Webster (Magnetes), Pitt Wilkinson (Philemus/Captain), Musicians: Lilian Evett, Sean Hooper, Mary Kroeber, Judy Webber, Martin Nicholls, Paul Nieman, Rory Allam, John Wesley Barker, Melinda Maxwell, Utako Ikeda
Directed by Peter Hall, Assistant to the Director John Heilpern, Designs by John Bury, Assistant Designer Timian Alsaker, Lighting by David Hersey, Music composed by Harrison Birtwistle, Music Direction Dominic Muldowney, Tape realisation Jonty Harrison

1976 TAMBURLAINE THE GREAT
by Christopher Marlowe

❝I was very impressed on Thursday night by the feeling of absolute evil that was unleashed in the auditorium. What we need to add now is a man who is constantly challenging God to prove Himself, to prove He exists. It is the first atheist play, and in a way the first existential play. It is utterly bleak and cynical.❞
Peter Hall (Peter Hall's Diaries)

❝The play draws you into Tamburlaine's ruthlessness, makes you one with it. You find yourself hoping that he will remain invincible; you do not want so perfect a pattern of victory to be spoiled. You do not even want him to be merciful, and spare those he has threatened with destruction; if he did that he would break his word and Tamburlaine is pre-eminently truthful.❞
Robert Cushman (Observer)

❝Albert Finney has the kind of physical authority that makes it credible he would use the Turkish Emperor as a footstool or would slit his son's throat for refusing to do battle. He ascends the staircase of tyrannical power with mellifluous assurance, baring his teeth with victorious venom as he crushes kings, and expressing with baffled awe the wonder that death could ultimately defeat him. It is a towering performance.❞
Milton Shulman (Evening Standard)

THE FORCE OF HABIT by Thomas Bernhard,
trans. by Neville and Stephen Plaice,
Dir. Elijah Moshinsky, Lyttelton 9.11.76
COUNTING THE WAYS by Edward Albee,
Dir. Bill Bryden, Olivier 6.12.76

> ❝What the play does is to give a picture of a society full of a sentimental romanticism that has just about reached bursting-point. There is, for instance, a brilliantly-staged picnic scene full of whirling parasols, boys with balloons, *La Bohème* on a wind-up gramophone and the constant strains of Strauss waltzes in the distance; and yet into this, like a shark at a festival, comes a militaristic law-student doing target practise against a tree. And there is an even more chilling moment in the voluptuous night-club cabaret scene when, amidst the semi-naked mermaids and the erotic shepherdesses, the patrons sing *Deutschland über Alles* overlooked by the epicene, green-faced compere on a plinth.❞
>
> *Michael Billington* (Guardian)

> ❝If this is a play for the 1970s, it is because Horváth did not know what was coming; and depicted a society of small shopkeepers, gamblers, and pensioned officers who are still getting along somehow even though the economic ground has been cut from under their feet. It is a spectacle of fear, bravado, impetuous one-night spending, and fear of tomorrow that supplies the all-too-obvious link.❞
>
> *Irving Wardle* (The Times)

> ❝An achievement little short of sensational – the first English production of a European masterpiece as theatrical as it is profound, as funny as it is cruel, and as perceptive as it is compassionate.❞
>
> *John Barber* (Daily Telegraph)

1977 TALES FROM THE VIENNA WOODS
by Ödön von Horváth, trans. by **Christopher Hampton**

CAST: Susan Williamson (*Alfred's Mother*), Stephen Rea (*Alfred*), Madoline Thomas (*Alfred's Grandmother*), Oliver Cotton (*Ferdinand von Hierlinger*), Elizabeth Spriggs (*Valerie*), Pitt Wilkinson (*Havlitschek*), Warren Clarke (*Oskar*), Nicholas Selby (*The Captain*), Vivienne Burgess (*The Lady*), Kate Nelligan (*Marianne*), Paul Rogers (*The Zauberkönig*), Rosamund Greenwood (*First Aunt*), Ann Way (*Second Aunt*), Struan Rodger (*Erich*), Rowena Shah (*Ida*), Toyah Willcox (*Emma*), Sylvia Coleridge (*Helene*), Anne Leon (*The Maid*), Ellen Pollock (*The Baroness*), John Gill (*The Confessor*), Brenda Blethyn (*The Girlfriend*), Timothy Block (*The Boyfriend*), Peter Carlisle (*The American*), Trevor Ray (*The Compere*), Diane Bates, Nicholas Frith, Trevor Goodall (*Children*), Shulie Bannister, Brenda Blethyn, Imogen Claire, Irene Gorst, Maya Kemp, Lucinda Macdonald (*Cabaret Girls*), Jonathan Battersby, Michael Beint, Edna Doré, Ray Edwards, Martin Friend, Glyn Grain, Brian Kent, Marianne Morley, Peter Needham, Rose Power, Daniel Thorndike (*Passers-by, waiters, guests at the tavern and Maxim's*)
Musicians: Emilio, Howard Evans, Alan Gout, Peter Jarvis, Gary Kettel, Garth Morton, Ernest Naser, Chris Nicholls, Mike Paige, Nigel Pinkett, Robert Stewart, Robin Williams, Nic Worters
Directed by Maximilian Schell, *Designed by* Timothy O'Brien and Tazeena Firth, *Lighting by* David Hersey, *Assistant to the Lighting Designer* Alan Jacobi, *Music arranged by* Robert Stewart, *Choreography by* Peter Walker

John Haynes

Left: **Stephen Rea** (Alfred), **Kate Nelligan** (Marianne), **Elizabeth Spriggs** (Valerie)

CAST: Michael Gough *(Ernest)*, Joan Hickson *(Delia)*, Michael Kitchen *(Nick)*, Polly Adams *(Jan)*, Derek Newark *(Malcolm)*, Susan Littler *(Kate)*, Stephen Moore *(Trevor)*, Maria Aitken *(Susannah)*
Directed by Alan Ayckbourn and Peter Hall,
Designed by Timothy O'Brien and Tazeena Firth,
Lighting by Peter Radmore

1977 BEDROOM FARCE
by Alan Ayckbourn

Below: **Michael Gough** (Ernest),
Joan Hickson (Delia)

❛People had said to me that I'd set plays everywhere but in the bedroom and I got to think about them and became fascinated by what people do in bedrooms – I don't mean all that ho, ho risqué stuff, but the curious pastimes people take up.❜
Alan Ayckbourn

❛First dress rehearsal this afternoon to an invited audience, mostly young from colleges. They were like wild beasts let out of a cage. From the first line they roared with laughter. The actors had actually to tame them.❜
Peter Hall (Peter Hall's Diaries)

❛Like Feydeau and Wedekind before him, Mr Ayckbourn is a uniquely funny chronicler of human and marital despair, and it comes therefore as no real shock that the closing moments of *Bedroom Farce* consist of a lady in the dark telling herself that there's nothing to be afraid of. There is of course everything to be afraid of, not least mankind's inhumanity to mankind: "This old trouble again, is it?" asks Joan Hickson, patting a bedspread, and instantly summarising a thousand sexless marriages.❜
Sheridan Morley (Punch)

Anthony Crickmay

STATE OF REVOLUTION by Robert Bolt,
Dir. Christopher Morahan, Lyttelton 18.5.77
FOUR TO ONE by Gawn Grainger,
Dir. Sebastian Graham-Jones, Cottesloe 18.5.77
TO THOSE BORN LATER by Bertolt Brecht,
Dir. Michael Kustow, Cottesloe 1.6.77

OLD MOVIES by Bill Bryden, Dir. Bill Bryden,
Cottesloe 16.6.77
THE MADRAS HOUSE by Harley Granville Barker,
Dir. William Gaskill, Olivier 22.6.77
THE CAMILLA RINGBINDER SHOW by Trevor Ray and
Richard Mangan, Dir. Sebastian Graham-Jones,
Cottesloe 1.7.77

BOW DOWN by Tony Harrison (writer) and
Harrison Birtwistle (music), Dir. Walter Donohue,
Cottesloe 5.7.77
SIR IS WINNING by Shane Connaughton,
Dir. Christopher Morahan, Cottesloe 25.8.77

Reg Wilson

Above: **Michael Medwin** (Corvino), **Paul Scofield** (Volpone), **Ben Kingsley** (Mosca)

Above right: **Morag Hood** (Celia), **Paul Scofield** (Volpone)

1977 VOLPONE
by Ben Jonson

❝No sooner has a lounge-suited Gielgud finished the prologue from a corner of the auditorium than the lights go up on the stage to reveal Paul Scofield in a rich, red brocaded gown hailing a new season of profitable deceit – "Good morning to the day; and next, my gold! Open the shrine that I may see my saint." You could not have better auguries than that for a happy evening. The satirical laughters of Jonson's *Volpone* are as fresh as if they had been written this year, and in this production under Peter Hall's mercurial direction they tumble out as swiftly as you could ask.❞
B. A. Young (Financial Times)

❝I have bathed in the juice of July flowers! I will go further. This classic comedy is more delicious than the milk of unicorns and panther's breath mixed with Cretan wines. Even these superlatives lifted from Volpone's seduction speech don't do full justice to the pleasure I felt at the National Theatre last night. With Paul Scofield in a red wig making his first appearance at the theatre, and with the whole company on the tips of their toes, Ben Jonson's cynical 17th-century account of avarice and deceit blazes into life.❞
Felix Barker (Evening News)

CAST: Paul Scofield *(Volpone),* Ben Kingsley *(Mosca),* David Rappaport *(Nano),* Imogen Claire *(Androgyno),* John-Angelo Messana *(Castrone),* Paul Rogers *(Voltore),* Hugh Paddick *(Corbaccio),* Michael Medwin *(Corvino),* John Gielgud *(Sir Politic Wouldbe),* Ian Charleson *(Peregrine),* Morag Hood *(Celia),* Ray Edwards *(Corvino's servant),* Warren Clark *(Bonario),* Elizabeth Spriggs *(Lady Wouldbe),* Irene Gorst, Lucinda Macdonald *(Lady Wouldbe's women),* Nicholas Selby *(First Avocatore),* Peter Needham *(Second Avocatore),* Brian Kent *(Third Avocatore),* Daniel Thorndike *(Fourth Avocatore),* Norman Claridge *(Notario),* Michael Beint *(First Merchant),* Martin Friend *(Second Merchant),* Stanley Lloyd *(Third Merchant)*
With: Jonathan Battersby, Robert Howard, Chris Hunter, Marianne Morley, Peter Rocca, Dennis Tynsley
Directed by Peter Hall, *Assistant to the Director* Stewart Trotter, *Settings by* John Bury, *Costumes by* Deirdre Clancy, *Lighting by* David Hersey, *Songs by* Harrison Birtwistle

1978

LARK RISE
by **Keith Dewhurst** from **Flora Thompson**'s book

CAST: John Barrett *(Old Price/Dick/Grandfather)*, Martin Carthy *(Mr Pridham/Sam/singer)*, Warren Clarke *(Boamer/Cheapjack)*, Shirley Collins *(singer)*, Edna Doré *(Mrs Peverill/Queenie/Macey)*, Caroline Embling *(Laura)*, Brian Glover *(Mr Morris/Jerry Parish/Gardener/ Landlord)*, Howard Goorney *(Stut/Twister/Algy/Tramp)*, Glyn Grain *(Fisher/John Price/Carrier)*, James Grant *(Albert Timms)*, Laurence Hardiman *(Edmund)*, Louisa Livingstone *(Martha Beamish/Polly)*, Mary Miller *(Emma Timms)*, Derek Newark *(Pumpkin/Doctor/Squire Bracewell)*, Trevor Ray *(Bishie/Postie)*, Dinah Stabb *(Mrs Blaby/Mrs Beamish/Garibaldi Jacket)*, John Tams *(Cockie/singer)*, June Watson *(Mrs Spicer/Old Sally/Mrs Miller/Miss Ellison/Mrs Andrews)*
The Albion Band: Peter Bullock, Howard Evans, Michael Gregory, Ashley Hutchings, Phil Pickett, John Tams, Graeme Taylor, Shirley Collins, David Busby
Directed by Bill Bryden and Sebastian Graham-Jones, *Designs by* William Dudley, *Lighting by* William Dudley and Laurence Clayton, *Music Director* Ashley Hutchings

Right: **The Harvest scene, with promenade audience**

'Over the auditorium of the National's Cottesloe Theatre last night stretched the wide Oxfordshire sky. A church steeple pricked the sky above the wheatfields. Slowly the aspect changed as day wore on and the hamlet went about its work in the placid noon of the 1880s. The whole of rural life is here in a child's wistful memory.'
J. C. Trewin (Birmingham Post)

'A detailed and colourful mosaic of village rite, custom and gossip against a backcloth of muscular folk rock music from the Albion Band . . . Down below you may be jostled by Laura and her young brother, Edmund, scampering through the dewy morning, or by the shining, avuncular figure of Brian Glover as a barrow boy . . . From above you can enjoy the patterns of men striding afield, scything a resolutely choreographed progress through smiling customers.'
Michael Coveney (Financial Times)

Michael Mayhew

Kate Nelligan (Susan Treherne), **Stephen Moore** (Raymond Brock)

Nobby Clark

'It is said playwrights do not create great roles for women any more. David Hare has proved them wrong. His new play contains the finest modern part any actress could conjure up in her wildest dreaming. And in Kate Nelligan Mr Hare and the National have an actress with the presence, the range and the power to meet its every challenge. Her performance is breathtaking, her triumph total. For this is Hare painting on the widest canvas, both political and human. His heroine and her life are a metaphor for England and its post-war demise.'
Jack Tinker (Daily Mail)

'In defining the gradual disintegration and reformation of one lady's spirit, Hare's message is that power rots but money rots faster: his world is one where it has taken six thousand civil servants to dismantle an Empire built by six hundred, and where an ex-Embassy staffer can look back in nostalgia because "say what you like about the Foreign Office, at least they were hypocrites; in the City they don't even try that." Mr Hare's message sent back from the outer reach of disillusion, is that finally the only dignity lies in being alone, since together we've managed to ruin even twenty years of peace.'
Sheridan Morley (Punch)

1978 PLENTY
by **David Hare**

CAST: Kate Nelligan *(Susan Treherne)*, Julie Covington *(Alice Park)*, Stephen Moore *(Raymond Brock)*, Paul Freeman *(Codename Lazar)*, Robert Ralph *(A Frenchman)*, Basil Henson *(Sir Leonard Darwin)*, David Schofield *(Mick)*, Gil Brailey *(Louise)*, Kristopher Kum *(Mr Aung)*, Me Me Lai *(Mrs Aung)*, Lindsay Duncan *(Dorcas Frey)*, Tom Durham *(John Begley)*, Frederick Treves *(Sir Andrew Charleson)*, Timothy Davies *(Another Frenchman)*
Directed by David Hare, *Settings by* Hayden Griffin, *Costumes by* Deirdre Clancy, *Assistant Designer (settings)* Peter Hartwell, *Lighting by* Rory Dempster, *Music by* Nick Bicât

---

DON JUAN COMES BACK FROM THE WAR
by Odön von Horváth, trans. by Christopher Hampton,
Dir. Stewart Trotter, Cottesloe 18.4.78
BRAND by Henrik Ibsen, trans. by Geoffrey Hill,
Dir. Christopher Morahan, Olivier 25.4.78
LOST WORLDS by Wilson John Haire, Dir. Robert Kidd,
Cottesloe 25.5.78

JEWS/ARABS by Ron Hutchinson,
Dir. Nikolas Simmonds, Cottesloe 1.6.78 (Workshop)
MACBETH by William Shakespeare, Dir. Peter Hall
with John Russell Brown, Olivier 6.6.78
AMERICAN BUFFALO by David Mamet,
Dir. Bill Bryden, Cottesloe 28.6.78

HAS "WASHINGTON" LEGS? by Charles Wood,
Dir. Geoffrey Reeves, Cottesloe 29.11.78
STRIFE by John Galsworthy, Dir. Christopher Morahan,
Olivier 30.11.78
HEROD by Paul Mills, Dir. Sebastian Graham-Jones,
Cottesloe 11.12.78

CAST: Michael Gambon *(Jerry),* Penelope Wilton *(Emma),* Daniel Massey *(Robert),* Artro Morris *(Waiter),* Glenn Williams *(Barman)*
Directed by Peter Hall, *Designed by* John Bury, *Assistant Designer* Sue Jenkinson, *Lighting by* John Bury

1978 BETRAYAL
by Harold Pinter

Daniel Massey (Robert), **Michael Gambon** (Jerry), **Penelope Wilton** (Emma)

Michael Mayhew

❝Pinter has constructed a Chinese box which intrigues us with its permutation of deceits. More important than a husband's betrayal of a wife, or vice versa, is a man's betrayal of his best friend. With uncanny accuracy, Pinter records the phrases that pass between lovers in suspicion, ecstasy and despair.❞
Milton Shulman *(Evening Standard)*

❝*Betrayal* is an exquisite play, brilliantly simple in form and courageous in its search for a poetry that turns banality into a melancholy beauty . . . Pinter tunnels backward in time, starting the play with a meeting between his adulterous lovers, Jerry and Emma, in 1977, two years after their seven-year affair has died. In nine scenes we move back and back through the stages of the affair, until the play ends with its beginning in the house of Emma's husband, Robert, who is Jerry's best friend: it's like watching a flower blossom backwards, its petals inexorably closing.❞
Jack Kroll *(Newsweek)*

❝The promises and excuses that account for so much of the dialogue between the sexes are exactly captured. So are the graduations of male camaraderie in a St. John's Wood world that time apparently has left untouched. "We never played squash" says Robert warily when Jerry protests his friendship.❞
Robert Cushman *(Observer)*

1979 UNDISCOVERED COUNTRY

by Arthur Schnitzler, in a version by **Tom Stoppard**

❝*Undiscovered Country* is rich with jokes and fancies and the underlying blackness of its meaning is achieved by drawing the audience into the elegant and brittle immoralism of the world and people it creates so as, in the end, to shock us more deeply about ourselves. There is no need to seek analogies between our own times and Vienna on the eve of war and imperial collapse in order to appreciate the universality of the Hofreiters amid their circle. But Schnitzler is brilliantly evocative of the decadent spirit and manners of that Vienna and as we, with keen interest, examine his pathology we are bound to look for clues. The source of the tragedy, perhaps, is the persistence of a code of values and of conduct among the dominant class which is singularly inappropriate for the needs of a society obliged to adapt and change. Schnitzler himself makes no such heavy-handed point, but it is the genius of this frothy and entertaining play that it should go so deep and so near the knuckle.**❞**
Peter Jenkins (Spectator)

CAST: Dorothy Tutin *(Genia Hofreiter)*, Janet Whiteside *(Kathi)*, Sara Kestelman *(Mrs Wahl)*, Emma Piper *(Erna Wahl)*, Greg Hicks *(Otto von Aigner)*, Michael Byrne *(Dr Franz Mauer)*, John Wood *(Friedrich Hofreiter)*, John Harding *(Paul Kreindl)*, Anna Carteret *(Adele Natter)*, Glyn Grain *(Demeter Stanzides)*, Brian Kent *(Mr Natter)*, Joyce Redman *(Mrs von Aigner)*, Peter Needham *(Rosenstock)*, Elliott Cooper *(First Hiker)*, Glyn Baker *(Second Hiker)*, William Sleigh *(Third Hiker)*, Mark Farmer *(Bellboy)*, David Browning *(Mr Schmidt)*, Jane Evers *(Mrs Schmidt)*, Roger Gartland *(Mr Serknitz)*, Michael Bryant *(Dr von Aigner)*, Fiona Gaunt *(Spanish Girl)*, Anne Sedgwick *(French Girl)*, Dermot Crowley *(Albertus Rhon)*, Susan Gilmore *(Italian maid)*, Nik Forster *(Head Waiter)*, Martyn Whitby *(Penn, a guide)*, Adam Norton *(Gustl Wahl)*, Marjorie Yates *(Mrs Rhon)*, Marianne Morley *(French Nanny)*, Grant Warnock, Sandra Osborn, Graham McGrath, Catherine Evitt *(The Natters' children)*
Musicians: Michael Dore, Jack Fleetcroft, Paul Frowde, Michael Hart, Raymond Mosley, Dennis Nesbitt, Andy Patterson, John White
Directed by Peter Wood, *Settings by* William Dudley, *Costumes by* David Walker, *Lighting by* Robert Bryan, *Music by* John White

❝Working on the play, I often felt as if I were driving up the M1 in a Triumph Stag and finding myself overtaken by a 1922 Bentley.**❞**
Tom Stoppard (quoted in Peter Hall's Diaries)

Below: **Emma Piper** (Erna Wahl), **Dorothy Tutin** (Genia Hofreiter), **John Wood** (Friedrich Hofreiter), **Sara Kestelman** (Mrs Wahl), **John Harding** (Paul Kreindl)

Donald Cooper

All the plays that opened in 1979:

A FAIR QUARREL by Thomas Middleton and William Rowley, Dir. William Gaskill, Olivier 8.2.79
THE LONG VOYAGE HOME by Eugene O'Neill, Dir. Bill Bryden, Cottesloe 20.2.79

THE FRUITS OF ENLIGHTENMENT by Lev Tolstoy, trans. by Michael Frayn, Dir. Christopher Morahan, Olivier 8.3.79
FOR SERVICES RENDERED by W. Somerset Maugham, Dir. Michael Rudman, Lyttelton 1.5.79
CLOSE OF PLAY by Simon Gray, Dir. Harold Pinter, Lyttelton 24.5.79

DISPATCHES from Michael Herr's book, adapted for stage by Bill Bryden and the Company, Dir. Bill Bryden, Cottesloe 6.6.79
UNDISCOVERED COUNTRY by Arthur Schnitzler in a version by Tom Stoppard, Dir. Peter Wood, Olivier 20.6.79

CAST: Doreen Mantle *(Linda)*, Warren Mitchell *(Willy Loman)*, David Baxt *(Happy)*, Stephen Greif *(Biff)*, Ursula Smith *(The Woman)*, Michael J Jackson *(Bernard)*, Harry Towb *(Charley)*, Harold Kasket *(Uncle Ben)*, Jerry Harte *(Howard Wagner)*, Mandie Joel *(Jenny)*, Ronnie Letham *(Stanley)*, Carole Harrison *(Miss Forsyth)*, Liz Goulding *(Letta)*, Jeffrey Chiswick *(Waiter)*
Musicians: Bob Burns, Duncan Campbell, Derek Gutteridge, Michael Hart, Arthur Soothill, John White
Directed by Michael Rudman, *Settings by* John Gunter, *Costumes by* Lindy Hemming, *Lighting by* Mick Hughes, *Music by* John White

1979
DEATH OF A SALESMAN
by Arthur Miller

❝The play has a lot of soft lines in it, and is quite dated. But Michael Rudman has directed against that, kept it hard, kept it rapid, and has really done a superb job. Warren Mitchell's performance is something I shall never forget. One of the half-dozen great bits of totally assimilated character acting I have seen.❞
Peter Hall (Peter Hall's Diaries)

❝The tragedy of Willy Loman's failure bites harder not so much because the poor, defeated salesman has run out of his time and has become crazed by his failure, but because dimly and fleetingly he understands what is wrong. The play is about the horror of shattered illusions, which is, perhaps, why it works so well today. Thirty years on we stand where Willy Loman stood, unable to go back, but faced with an unspeakable future.❞
Barry Took (Punch)

❝Destroying the commodity values of the American dream, utterly painful in its depiction of one life gone rotten with false hopes, self-ignorance and finally familial hypocrisy, Miller's masterpiece is most memorable for its compassion and tenderness, for its clear-sighted affirmation of the essential goodness of common, put-upon, shat-upon humanity.❞
Steve Grant (Time Out)

Warren Mitchell (Willy Loman)

John Haynes

AS YOU LIKE IT by William Shakespeare, Dir. John Dexter, Olivier 1.8.79
WINGS by Arthur Kopit, Dir. John Madden, Cottesloe 15.8.79
DEATH OF A SALESMAN by Arthur Miller, Dir. Michael Rudman, Lyttelton 20.9.79

RICHARD III by William Shakespeare, Dir. Christopher Morahan, Olivier 4.10.79
AMADEUS by Peter Shaffer, Dir. Peter Hall, Olivier 2.11.79
CANDLEFORD by Keith Dewhurst from Flora Thompson's book, Dir. Bill Bryden and Sebastian Graham-Jones, Cottesloe 14.11.79

WHEN WE ARE MARRIED by J. B. Priestley, Dir. Robin Lefevre, Lyttelton 12.12.79
THE WILD DUCK by Henrik Ibsen, Dir. Christopher Morahan, Olivier 13.12.79

Nobby Clark

Paul Scofield (Salieri)

Simon Callow (Mozart), **Paul Scofield** (Salieri)

❝Simon Callow as Mozart goes to the harpsichord and astonishes everyone by playing a march just composed by Salieri. Then, under his fingers, Mozart adjusts the pedestrian little tune until it melts into the delicious *Non piu andrai* from *Figaro*. You can feel Salieri's glassy appreciation turn into black bile within him.❞
John Barber (Daily Telegraph)

CAST: Dermot Crowley, Donald Gee *(The 'Venticelli'),* Philip Locke *(Ignaz Breybig),* Paul Scofield *(Antonio Salieri),* Basil Henson *(Johann Kilian von Strack),* Andrew Cruickshank *(Count Orsini-Rosenberg),* Nicholas Selby *(Baron von Swieten),* Felicity Kendal *(Constanze Weber),* Simon Callow *(Wolfgang Amadeus Mozart),* William Sleigh *(Major Domo),* John Normington *(Joseph II)* Nik Forster, David Morris, Adam Norton, Steven Slater *(Servants)*
Glyn Baker, Nigel Bellairs, Terry Diab, Leo Dove, Jane Evers, Sandra Fehr, Robin McDonald, Peggy Marshall, Robin Meredith, Glenn Williams *(Citizens of Vienna)*
Directed by Peter Hall, *Design and lighting by* John Bury, *Assistant Designer* Sue Jenkinson, *Music by* Mozart and Salieri, *Music Direction by* Harrison Birtwistle, *Tape* Jonty Harrison, *Forte-piano played by* Christopher Kite

1979 AMADEUS
by Peter Shaffer

❝Peter's script is tougher, more precise and more personal than anything he has done before. In one way, he is writing about how he sees himself and his uncertainties compared to, say, Sam Beckett. The *nature* of talent, of art, comes winging through.❞
Peter Hall (Peter Hall's Diaries)

❝From the first preview there was never any question that, whatever the critics might say, the effect of the play on the public was going to be enormous. Playing it I had again the experience I've only had on two or three previous occasions: a hunger from the audience, a feeling that they were getting something they'd done without for too long.❞
Simon Callow (Being an Actor)

❝Scofield's Salieri is a man who has been rewarded for his conformity with fame and riches in his lifetime but knows he leaves behind only mediocrity. In Scofield's towering performance only the passion of jealousy breaks through the courtly mask. And that most corroding of emotions proves as deadly as arsenic to both Mr. Shaffer's compelling protagonists.❞ *Jack Tinker (Daily Mail)*

Right: **Michael Gambon** (Galileo), **Nicholas Selby** (Sagredo)

1980

THE LIFE OF GALILEO
by **Bertolt Brecht**, trans. by **Howard Brenton**

CAST: Melvyn Bedford *(Second secretary)*, Michael Beint *(Mathematician/Philippo Mucius)*, Nigel Bellairs *(Senator/Monk)*, Edmund Bennett *(Court Chamberlain)*, Marc Brenner *(Andrea Sarti as a boy/Second Boy)*, Selina Cadell *(Virginia)*, Simon Callow *(Fulganzio)*, Elliott Cooper *(Ludovico Marsili)*, Andrew Cruickshank *(Signor Priuli)*, Peter Dawson *(First secretary)*, Mark Dignam *(Cardinal Bellarmin)*, Sandra Fehr *(The Ballad Singer's Wife)*, Michael Gambon *(Galileo Galilei)*, Roger Gartland *(First Astronomer/Cosimo de'Medici)*, Peter Harding *(Door Keeper)*, James Hayes *(Federzoni)*, Basil Henson *(Cardinal Barberini (Pope Urban VIII))*, Robert Howard *(Philosopher/High Official)*, Brian Kent *(Father Christopher Clavius)*, Peter Land *(The Ballad Singer)*, Harry Lomax *(Very old Cardinal)*, Kenneth Mackintosh *(Signor Vanni)*, Peggy Marshall *(Lady in Waiting)*, Artro Morris *(Fat Prelate)*, Peter Needham *(Second Astronomer/Signor Mincio)*, Adam Norton *(Thin Monk)*, Timothy Norton *(Cosimo de'Medici as a boy)*, Robert Oates *(The Speaker)*, Robert Ralph *(Cardinal's Monk)*, Norman Rutherford *(The Doge of Venice)*, Nicholas Selby *(Sagredo)*, William Sleigh *(An individual)*, Adam Stafford *(First Boy)*, Jill Stanford *(Younger Lady in Waiting)*, David Stone *(Third Boy)*, Michael Thomas *(Andrea Sarti as a young man)*, Daniel Thorndike *(Philosopher)*, Gordon Whiting *(Theologian/Clerk)*, Glenn Williams *(Scholar/Frontier Guard)*
With: Terry Diab, Jane Evers, Michael Fenner, Michelle Middleton, Stephen Rooney, Janet Whiteside
Musicians: Boys of the John Paul Foundation *Music Director* John East, *with* Andrew Findon, John Harle, Kevin Leeman
Directed by John Dexter, *Settings by* Jocelyn Herbert, *Costumes by* Jocelyn Herbert and Stephen Skaptason, *Lighting by* Andy Phillips, *Music by* Hanns Eisler, *Music Director* Dominic Muldowney

Zoë Dominic

❛Brecht admired English writing. We have an informal tradition which he was trying to inject into his own German text. The result is great formal language with a dirty underbelly.❜
Howard Brenton (quoted in *Theatre at Work* by Jim Hiley, 1981)

❛*The Life of Galileo* shows the National at the peak of its powers. Directed by John Dexter, the production imaginatively fills the open stage of the Olivier with sophisticated stage machinery and superbly-articulated performances . . . But the heart of this amazingly vital production beats in the title role by Michael Gambon. His is a tremendous accomplishment in acting.❜
Richard Christiansen (Chicago Tribune)

❛Gambon gives a performance which places him at the height of his profession: a richly detailed characterisation, layer on layer of fallibly fleshed humanity using every twisting compromise to stay alive, at once justifying and castigating Galileo.❜
John James (Times Educational Supplement)

All the plays that opened in 1980:

HUGHIE by Eugene O'Neill, Dir. Bill Bryden, Cottesloe 22.1.80
THEE AND ME by Philip Martin, Dir. Michael Rudman, Lyttelton 26.2.80

THE ICEMAN COMETH by Eugene O'Neill, Dir. Bill Bryden, Cottesloe 4.3.80
OTHELLO by William Shakespeare, Dir. Peter Hall, Olivier 20.3.80
EARLY DAYS by David Storey, Dir. Lindsay Anderson, Cottesloe 22.4.80

THE BROWNING VERSION and HARLEQUINADE by Terence Rattigan, Dir. Michael Rudman, Lyttelton 13.5.80
SISTERLY FEELINGS by Alan Ayckbourn, Dir. Alan Ayckbourn and Christopher Morahan, Olivier 3/4.6.80

Foreground: Gina Bellman (Susanna Walcott), **Caroline Embling** (Abigail Williams), **Tracy Taylor** (Mercy Lewis), **Colette Barker** (Betty Parris)

Background: Tony Haygarth (Deputy Governor Danforth), **Dave Hill** (Rev Samuel Parris), **Derek Newark** (Thomas Putnam), **John Tams** (Marshall Herrick), **Stephen Petcher** (Hopkins)

Michael Mayhew

❛I can almost tell what the political situation in a country is when *The Crucible* is suddenly a hit there – it is either a warning of tyranny on the way or a reminder of tyranny just past.❜ *Arthur Miller*

❛Possibly the best American play of this century.❜ *B. A. Young (Financial Times)*

❛Mr Bryden's production moves with so powerful a forward thrust that, at the close, one is hardly aware that one has been almost 3½ hours in the theatre. The shrill and shivering dementia of the pubescent girls, the priest who, though sincerely believing in demonic possession, comes to see the terrible injustice of what is being perpet-rated; above all, the essential goodness, for all their imperfections, of the farmer Proctor and his wife.❜ *Francis King (S. Telegraph)*

❛When Abigail screams chillingly, claiming to see a yellow bird menacing her, more than one member of the audience turned to see where she pointed.❜
David Scott Kastan (Times Lit. Supp.)

1980 THE CRUCIBLE
by Arthur Miller

CAST: Dave Hill *(Rev. Samuel Parris)*, Colette Barker *(Betty Parris)*, Isabelle Lucas *(Tituba)*, Caroline Embling *(Abigail Williams)*, Gina Bellman *(Susanna Walcott)*, Anne Kristen *(Goodwife Ann Putman)*, Derek Newark *(Thomas Putnam)*, Tracy Taylor *(Mercy Lewis)*, Valerie Whittington *(Mary Warren)*, Mark McManus *(John Proctor)*, Edna Doré *(Goodwife Rebecca Nurse)*, J G Devlin *(Giles Corey)*, James Grant *(Rev. John Hale)*, Dinah Stabb *(Goodwife Elizabeth Proctor)*, Alex McCrindle *(Francis Nurse)*, Barrie Rutter *(Ezekiel Cheever)*, John Tams *(Marshall Herrick)*, Jeffrey Chiswick *(Judge Hathorne)*, Tony Haygarth *(Deputy Governor Danforth)*, Peggy Marshall *(Sarah Good)*, Stephen Petcher *(Hopkins)*
Director Bill Bryden, *Settings* Hayden Griffin, *Costumes* Deirdre Clancy, *Lighting* Rory Dempster, *Music* John Tams

James Carter (Nawadaha), **Frederick Warder** (Hiawatha)

Laurence Burns

1980

HIAWATHA
by **Longfellow**, adapted by **Michael Bogdanov**

CAST: James Carter *(Nawadaha),* William Sleigh *(Gitche Manito),* Yvonne Bryceland *(Nokomis),* Robert Oates *(Mudjekeewin),* Frederick Warder *(Hiawatha),* John Normington *(Iagoo),* Joss Buckley *(Chibiabos),* Michael Fenner *(Kwasind),* Jane Evers *(Kwasind's Mother),* Terry Diab *(Minnehaha),* Jeff Teare *(Pau-Puk-Keewis),* Michael Gregory *(Drums) Directed by* Michael Bogdanov, *Designs by* Marty Flood, *Lighting by* Chris Ellis, *Music and dance by* Jeff Teare, *Voice* Jenny Patrick, *Movement by* Frederick Warder

❝Using the simplest of props, Bogdanov achieves scenes of extraordinary richness and beauty. A river is created by the Indian-garbed actors slowly moving poles up and down for Hiawatha to swim through. And Minnehaha is transformed into a maize plant simply by wrapping green and yellow ribbons round her. The show is half theatre, half circus with the energetic company dancing, chanting, juggling and beating out frenzied rhythms on both tom-toms and a huge, circular drum. But this splendidly boisterous energy does nothing to obscure the more poignant moments. Minnehaha's death in bleak midwinter – the actors conjure up a snowstorm simply by waving white cloths through the air – is memorably moving and the production never loses sight of the Indian's mystically close relationship to nature and the elements. A feeling of ritual and innocent wonder dominate the performance and I find it hard to imagine a more thrilling introduction to the theatre for young children.❞
Charles Spencer (New Standard)

❝This is excellent Hiawatha
Children cheering, every one.
Theatre like this lifts the spirit,
Why can't adults have such fun?❞
Michael Billington (Guardian)

THE CARETAKER by Harold Pinter, Dir. Kenneth Ives, Lyttelton 11.11.80
HIAWATHA by Longfellow, adapted by Michael Bogdanov, Dir. Michael Bogdanov, Olivier 10.12.80

1981 MAN AND SUPERMAN
by Bernard Shaw

❝Prepare yourself to face a trumpery story of modern London life, a life in which, as you know, the ordinary man's main business is to get means to keep up the position and habits of a gentleman, and the ordinary woman's business is to get married.❞
Bernard Shaw

❝Apart from being visually resplendent, with a great arch of silver foil reflecting the green-and-orange of southern Spain, this production also does justice to Shaw's ceaseless wit (the Devil suavely announces that "the gate here always opens to the repentant prodigal") and to the beguiling music of his prose.❞
Michael Billington (Guardian)

❝The complete version reveals the Shavian alter ego of Mendoza The Devil as second only to the role of Tanner. Michael Bryant, in a vast sombrero, first appears as the silkiest of brigands, holding a contentious crew of anarchists and social democratic outlaws in the palm of his hand; and then presents an extremely gentlemanly Prince of Darkness. The production brilliantly seizes on Mendoza's recollections of waitering at the Savoy to bring on the Devil as a head waiter.❞
Irving Wardle (The Times)

CAST: Basil Henson *(Roebuck Ramsden)*, Janet Whiteside *(Parlourmaid)*, Timothy Davies *(Octavius Robinson)*, Daniel Massey *(John Tanner)*, Penelope Wilton *(Ann Whitefield)*, Antonia Pemberton *(Mrs Whitefield)*, Barbara Hicks *(Miss Ramsden)*, Anna Carteret *(Violet Robinson)*, James Carter *(Henry Straker)*, Greg Hicks *(Hector Malone)*, Michael Bryant *(Mendoza)*, Daniel Thorndike *(The Anarchist)*, Peter Dawson *(Rowdy Social-Democrat)*, Brian Kent *(Sulky Social-Democrat)*, Philip Dunbar *(Duval)*, Norman Rutherford *(The Goatherd)*, Nicholas Geake *(Spanish Captain)*, Nigel Bellairs, Robert Oates, Robert Ralph, Glenn Williams *(Brigands)*, David Cameron, Stephen Hattersley, Christopher Snell, Charles Wegner *(Spanish Army)*, Peter Welch *(Irishman)*
Directed by Christopher Morahan, *Settings by* Ralph Koltai, *Costumes by* David Walker, *Lighting by* Joe Davis, *Music by* Dominic Muldowney, *Voice by* Jenny Patrick

Donald Cooper

Left: **Daniel Massey** (John Tanner), **Penelope Wilton** (Anne Whitefield)

All the plays that opened in 1981:

MAN AND SUPERMAN by Bernard Shaw,
Dir. Christopher Morahan, Olivier 22.1.81
THE TICKET-OF-LEAVE MAN by Tom Taylor,
Dir. Piers Haggard, Cottesloe 12.2.81

A MONTH IN THE COUNTRY by Ivan Turgenev,
trans. by Isaiah Berlin, Dir. Peter Gill, Olivier 19.2.81
DON JUAN by Molière, trans. by John Fowles,
Dir. Peter Gill, Cottesloe 7.4.81
MEASURE FOR MEASURE by William Shakespeare,
Dir. Michael Rudman, Lyttelton 14.4.81

SERJEANT MUSGRAVE'S DANCE by John Arden,
Dir. John Burgess, Cottesloe 27.5.81
THE SHOEMAKER'S HOLIDAY by Thomas Dekker,
Dir. John Dexter, Olivier 19.6.81
ONE WOMAN PLAYS by Dario Fo and Franca Rame,
version by Olwen Wymark, Dir. Michael Bogdanov,
Cottesloe 18.6.81

CAST: Derek Newark (Rebolledo), Robert Oates (First Soldier), Michael Fenner (Second Soldier), Iain Rattray (Third Soldier), Stephen Hattersley (Fourth Soldier), Martin Garfield (Fifth Soldier), Russell Kilmister (Sixth Soldier), Yvonne Bryceland (Chispa), Daniel Massey (Captain don Alvaro de Ataide), Michael Beint (Sergeant), Daniel Thorndike (Don Mendo), Peter Løvstrøm (Nuno), Terry Diab (Ines), Leslee Udwin (Isabel), Michael Bryant (Pedro Crespo), Clive Arrindell (Juan), Jane Evers (Ginesa), Glenn Williams (Servant to Crespo), Basil Henson (Don Lope de Figueroa), Nigel Bellairs (Clerk), Nicholas Selby (Philip II)
Musicians: Arthur Soothill, Peter Howe, Richard Nairn, Eddie Thompson, Ivan Trueman, Olav Vas
Directed by Michael Bogdanov, Designs by Stephanie Howard, Lighting by Andrew Torble and Michael Bogdanov, Music by John White, Fight Direction by Malcolm Ranson, Voice by Jenny Patrick

1981

THE MAYOR OF ZALAMEA
by **Calderon**, trans. by **Adrian Mitchell**

Right: **Leslee Udwin** (Isabel), **Michael Bryant** (Pedro Crespo), **Clive Arrindell** (Juan)

Laurence Burns

❛In this play alone Calderon was coming to grips with the very metal of the human condition . . . Honour here is everything. When a swaggering army captain rapes the beautiful daughter of a proud, rich peasant, and then tries to skulk behind his noble birth and army rank to escape the wrath of civilian law, the play pulls no punches. The Best Garrotting Ever Done is the prophetic sub-title.❜
Jack Tinker (Daily Mail)

❛The vitality of the characters in Calderon's play provides them with facets of personality that are at once comical and serious. The captain blindly pursues his prejudice that peasant women are ugly until the mere glimpse of Crespo's daughter obsesses him. Crespo and the general of the Spanish army are blindly prideful to the point of laughter, and both pride and prejudice tip the balance to murder, rape and revenge, after provoking laughter through mock-heroic swordfights and exchanges of insults.❜
Ned Chaillet (The Times)

❛The great virtue of Michael Bogdanov's production is the care it takes over the shifting perspectives on honour: that and the vigour with which the cast transforms the ideas and actions . . . Michael Bryant, sly and pragmatic as well as fanatical, flares magnificently when, finding a new pride in dogged self-abasement, he confronts his tormentor, played with poisonous, mellifluous arrogance by Daniel Massey.❜
Robert Cushman (Observer)

Greg Hicks (Orestes)

Nobby Clark

"The victory of father-right over mother-right is the social pendulum of this trilogy. To have women play women in our production would have seemed as if we in the 20th century were smugly assuming that the sex war was over and that the oppressions of the patriarchal code exist only in past centuries. The maleness of the piece is like a vacuum-sealed container keeping this ancient issue fresh."
Tony Harrison

"Again and again one is startled and enthralled. As when skyscraper-high doors open to reveal the corpses of Cassandra and Agamemnon, his arm raised, frozen in rigor mortis. Or when Orestes first enters, supremely graceful, looking like a Japanese prince . . . Or when the Furies surround and absorb Orestes, as in the slime of a spider's web. Or the wonderful conclusion, when the actors make us all stand, and parade through us, ritualistically, while a living torch flame symbolises the coming of enlightenment."
John Barber (Daily Telegraph)

"The central drama, a titanic contest between blood-loyalty and the loyalties of the human bond emerges in letters a mile high. So does the figure of Clytemnestra as the dominating presence in a community that despises women. The production articulates such ideas in scenes such as Agamemnon's masterly, contemptuous return from Troy."
Irving Wardle (The Times)

CAST: Sean Baker, David Bamber, James Carter, Timothy Davies, Peter Dawson, Philip Donaghy, Roger Gartland, James Hayes, Greg Hicks, Kenny Ireland, Alfred Lynch, John Normington, Tony Robinson, David Roper, Barrie Rutter, Michael Thomas *(Chorus and other speaking parts)* Nigel Bellairs, Mark Bond, Martin Garfield, Peter Gerald, John Gill, Colin Haigh, Peter Hale, Robert Howard, Graham Pountney, Robert Ralph, Norman Rutherford, Leslie Southwick, Glenn Williams,

Richard Williams *(Anti-chorus)*
Musicians: Malcolm Bennett, Simon Limbrick, Ben Mason, Helen Tunstall, Rory Allam, John Harle, Jim Rae, Arthur Soothill, Brian Ackerman
Directed by Peter Hall, *Music by* Harrison Birtwistle, *Designs by* Jocelyn Herbert, *Assistant to the Designer* Sue Jenkinson, *Lighting by* John Bury, *Movement by* Stuart Hopps, *Musical Direction by* Malcolm Bennett, *Voice by* Jane Manning

1981

THE ORESTEIA
trilogy by **Aeschylus**, in a version by **Tony Harrison**

THE ORESTEIA the trilogy by Aeschylus in a version by Tony Harrison, Dir. Peter Hall, music by Harrison Birtwistle, Olivier 28.10.81
TRUE WEST by Sam Shepard, Dir. John Schlesinger, Cottesloe 9.12.81

THE SECOND MRS TANQUERAY by Arthur W. Pinero, Dir. Michael Rudman, Lyttelton 15.12.81

Nobby Clark

Left: **Bob Hoskins** (Lee). *Below:* **Antony Sher** (Austin)

1981
TRUE WEST
by Sam Shepard

CAST: Bob Hoskins *(Lee),* Antony Sher *(Austin),* Shane Rimmer *(Saul Kimmer),* Patricia Hayes *(Mom)*
Directed by John Schlesinger, *Designs by* Grant Hicks, *Lighting by* Rory Dempster

❝It is out of the myths, dreams and fantasies of American life that Sam Shepard moulds his plays. From the heaps of images that clutter up the media and culture of Americana, Shepard fashions anecdotes like a sculptor scrabbling for his material in a junk-pile.❞
Milton Shulman (Standard)

❝They are brothers reflecting two sides of Shepard himself; Austin a middle-class screen-writer, and Lee a wild vagabond who lives in the desert scratching an existence out of dog-fighting and petty crime. Coming together after years apart, they are first seen jockeying for status on the neutral territory of their mother's house.❞
Irving Wardle (The Times)

❝The brute turns writer, the writer brute. This triggers a performance explosion by Bob Hoskins as Lee and Antony Sher as Austin. We are now told about their father, a pathetic destitute who lost his false teeth in a bag of chop suey on a bar crawl with the younger son. For the first time Austin has a story that rivals the real experience of his brother; Lee, trying to concentrate at the typewriter, assaults the machine with a golf club. The writing begins to expand in a series of violent images . . . Finally Mom arrives in a blonde perm with matching luggage.❞
Michael Coveney (Financial Times)

'It's about time the National Theatre got round to staging the real classics; and having finally taken the plunge with *Guys and Dolls* they have surfaced with a production that for sheer brazen pleasure is unequalled in London.'
Robert Cushman (Observer)

'The acting in even the small parts is really acting, never simply leading up to the next number . . . There is literally never a dull moment. To quote from Sarah's song of freshly-released affection, if I were a bell, I'd be ringing.'
B. A. Young (Financial Times)

'This is the American musical at its best. And the National Theatre at its best. Consider yourself lucky if you get a ticket, for this is bound to be the hottest show in town.'
Arthur Thirkell (Daily Mirror)

CAST: Barrie Rutter *(Benny Southstreet),* David Healy *(Nicely-Nicely Johnson),* Kevin Williams *(Rusty Charley),* Julie Covington *(Sarah),* John Normington *(Arvide Abernathy),* Rachel Izen *(Agatha),* Robert Ralph *(Calvin),* Belinda Sinclair *(Martha),* Bill Paterson *(Harry the Horse),* Harry Towb *(Lieutenant Brannigan),* Bob Hoskins *(Nathan Detroit),* Norman Warwick *(Angie the Ox),* Richard Walsh *(Scranton Slim),* Kevin Quarmby *(Joey Perhaps),* Robert Ralph *(Regret),* William Armstrong *(Society Max),* Larrington Walker *(Liverlips Louis),* Bernard Sharpe *(Hot Horse Herbie),* Mark Bond *(Sky Rocket),* Julia McKenzie *(Miss Adelaide),* Sally Cooper, Fiona Hendley *(Hot Box Girls)* Ian Charleson *(Sky Masterson),* Robert Oates *(Voice of Joey Biltmore),* William Armstrong *(Master of Ceremonies),* Rachel Izen, Belinda Sinclair *(More Hot Box Girls),* Imelda Staunton *(Mimi),* Irlin Hall *(General Cartwright),* James Carter *(Big Jule),* Norman Warwick *(Drunk),* Kevin Williams *(Waiter in the Hot Box)*
The Choo-Choo Boys Band: Tony Britten, Terry Davies, Lenny Bush, Mitch Dalton, Martin Drover, Howard Evans, Andy Findon, Ian Green, John

1982

GUYS AND DOLLS
based on **Damon Runyon**, musics and lyrics by **Frank Loesser**, book by **Jo Swerling** and **Abe Burrows**

Harle, Paul Nieman, Bobby Orr, Steve Saunders, Ray Warleigh, David White
Directed by Richard Eyre, *Musical staging by* David Toguri, *Music arrangements by* Tony Britten and Terry Davies, *Settings by* John Gunter, *Costumes by* Sue Blane, *Lighting by* David Hersey, *Dialect Coach* Joan Washington

John Haynes

Finale

All the plays that opened in 1982:

SUMMER by Edward Bond, Dir. Edward Bond, Cottesloe 27.1.82

GUYS AND DOLLS based on a story and characters of Damon Runyon, music and lyrics by Frank Loesser, Book by Jo Swerling and Abe Burrows, Dir. Richard Eyre, choreography by David Toguri, MD Tony Britten, Olivier 9.3.82

THE PRINCE OF HOMBURG by Heinrich von Kleist in a version by John James, Dir. John Burgess, Cottesloe 22.4.82

UNCLE VANYA by Anton Chekhov in a version by Pam Gems, Dir. Michael Bogdanov, Lyttelton 18.5.82

'Mr Eyre's staging says everything there is to know about a society where each man has his price. Pockmarked bawds, a rapacious beanpole Polly Peachum and a murderous Lucy Lockit, leave us in no doubt about the sort of company Captain Macheath keeps when he is at home. Paul Jones makes sure we have a Macheath who is a match for all these unlovely sluts. A mean-eyed Glasgow chauvinist, who takes his pleasure where he may, and gives his lusts the urgency of a man who knows full well his days may be numbered, it is a powerfully-judged performance, which he stands and delivers.'
Jack Tinker (Daily Mail)

'When David Ryall's morose Lockit puts on his boots, the putting on of the boots becomes an absorbing activity. When a bosom is bared or soup splashed about, these things become more than theatrical symbols: they are tangible necessities. The production absorbs eclectically, every suggestion from Cruikshank to Toulouse-Lautrec appropriate to the moment. The dust, the sour erotic grimace, the sweat, the saucers of tea, the juggling, the bad teeth: excellent characterisation is accompanied by inventive and patient realism (and beautifully timed stage business) which roots Gay's moral insights in an actual world of shabby ambition and pathetic acquisitiveness.'
John Fuller (Times Literary Supplement)

John Haynes

Paul Jones (Macheath)

1982 THE BEGGAR'S OPERA
by John Gay

CAST: William Armstrong *(Beggar),* Norman Warwick *(First Gentleman),* Kevin Williams *(Pickpocket),* Kevin Quarmby *(Second Gentleman),* David Ryall *(Fence),* Harry Towb *(Irish Cockney sneak thief),* Paul Jones *(Pimp),* Harry Towb *(Peachum),* Kevin Williams *(Filch),* June Watson *(Mrs Peachum),* Belinda Sinclair *(Polly Peachum),* Paul Jones *(Macheath),* Larrington Walker *(Ben Budge),* Richard Walsh *(Matt of the Mint),* William Armstrong *(Jemmy Twitcher),* Norman Warwick *(Crook-fingered Jack),* Kevin Williams *(Wat Dreary),* Kevin Quarmby *(Nimming Ned),* Vincent Pickering *(Harry Paddington/Drawer),* Fiona Hendley *(Jenny Diver),* Gail Rolfe *(Mrs Coaxer),* Rachel Izen *(Mrs Vixen),* Imelda Staunton *(Molly Brazen),* Belinda Sinclair *(Dolly Trull),* Sally Cooper *(Suky Tawdry),* June Watson *(Mrs Slammekin),* David Ryall *(Lockit),* Imelda Staunton *(Lucy Lockit),* Irlin Hall *(Mrs Trapes),* Kevin Quarmby *(Gaoler)*
Musicians: Rory Allam, Robin Jeffrey, Tim Laycock, Roderick Skeaping
Directed by Richard Eyre, *Designs by* John Gunter, *Music adapted by* Dominic Muldowney, *Dances by* David Toguri, *Lighting by* Peter Radmore, *Dialect coach* Joan Washington

DON QUIXOTE a play by Keith Dewhurst from the novel by Miguel de Cervantes, Dir. Bill Bryden, Olivier 18.6.82
THE BEGGAR'S OPERA by John Gay, Dir. Richard Eyre, Cottesloe 1.7.82

DANTON'S DEATH by Georg Buchner in a version by Howard Brenton, Dir. Peter Gill, Olivier 21.7.82
THE CAUCASIAN CHALK CIRCLE by Bertolt Brecht, trans. by James and Tania Stern with W. H. Auden, Dir. Michael Bogdanov and Justin Greene, Cottesloe 2.8.82 (NT Education presentation)

THE IMPORTANCE OF BEING EARNEST by Oscar Wilde, Dir. Peter Hall, Lyttelton 16.9.82
THE SPANISH TRAGEDY by Thomas Kyd, Dir. Michael Bogdanov, Cottesloe 22.9.82

Above: **Nigel Havers** (Algernon Moncrieff), **Martin Jarvis** (John Worthing);

Below: **Zoë Wanamaker** (Gwendolen Fairfax), **Elizabeth Garvie** (Cecily Cardew)

Zoe Dominic

Judi Dench (Lady Bracknell)

❝Exquisitely trivial, a delicate bubble of fancy, and it has its philosophy: we should treat all the trivial things of life very seriously and all the serious things of life with sincere and studied triviality❞
Oscar Wilde

❝Hall has discovered something of importance about *The Importance*, which is that if it is played with immense solemnity by people for whom muffins are a way of life and cucumber sandwiches no laughing matter, then it becomes an even funnier play.❞
Sheridan Morley (Punch)

❝For Judi Dench's performance as Lady Bracknell I have almost nothing but praise, in abundance . . . She is formidably funny, with finger-tip control of nuclear comic energy; needing only to remove her spectacles when she comes to the notorious handbag line. Here is a definitive Lady Bracknell.❞
Richard Findlater (Plays and Players)

❝Peter Hall has directed and John Bury sumptuously mounted a production worthy to stand beside the best history can offer.❞
Tom Vaughan (Morning Star)

1982 THE IMPORTANCE OF BEING EARNEST
by Oscar Wilde

CAST: Nigel Havers *(Algernon Moncrieff)*, Brian Kent *(Lane)*, Martin Jarvis *(John Worthing)*, Judi Dench *(Lady Bracknell)*, Zoë Wanamaker *(Gwendolen Fairfax)*, Anna Massey *(Miss Prism)*, Elizabeth Garvie *(Cecily Cardew)*, Paul Rogers *(Rev Canon Chasuble)*, John Gill *(Merriman)*, Alan Haywood *(Footman)*
Directed by Peter Hall, *Design and lighting by* John Bury, *Assistant Designer* Sue Jenkinson

---

SCHWEYK IN THE SECOND WORLD WAR
by Bertolt Brecht, trans. by Susan Davies, music by
Hanns Eisler, Dir. Richard Eyre, Olivier 23.9.82

WAY UPSTREAM by Alan Ayckbourn,
Dir. Alan Ayckbourn, Lyttelton 4.10.82
OTHER PLACES three plays by Harold Pinter:
Family Voices, Victoria Station, A Kind of Alaska,
Dir. Peter Hall, Cottesloe 14.10.82

MAJOR BARBARA by Bernard Shaw, Dir. Peter Gill,
Lyttelton 27.10.82
A MIDSUMMER NIGHT'S DREAM
by William Shakespeare, Dir. Bill Bryden,
Cottesloe 25.11.82

1983

THE RIVALS
by Richard Brinsley Sheridan

CAST: Barry James (Fag), Steven Law (Coachman), Sabina Franklyn (Lucy), Anne Louise Lambert (Lydia Languish), Fiona Shaw (Julia Melville), Geraldine McEwan (Mrs Malaprop), Michael Hordern (Sir Anthony Absolute), Patrick Ryecart (Captain Jack Absolute), Edward Petherbridge (Faulkland), Tim Curry (Bob Acres), David Hitchen (Errand boy), Niall Buggy (Sir Lucius O'Trigger), Philip Talbot (David), Brian Kent (Tailor), Marianne Morley (Housekeeper), Kate Gielgud (Maid), Douglas Fielding (Wig Master), Michael Mascoll (Blackamoor), Pauline Cadell, Stephen Gordon, Paul Stewart (Servants)
Musicians: Charles Duncan, Neil Fairbairn, Timothy Homfray, Melinda Maxwell, Malcolm Ross
Directed by Peter Wood, Settings by John Gunter, Costumes by Bruce Snyder, Lighting by Robert Bryan, Music by Dominic Muldowney, Assistant Designers Sue Jenkinson and Chris Townsend

Michael Hordern
(Sir Anthony Absolute)

Zoe Dominic

Geraldine McEwan
(Mrs Malaprop)

❝Style, as distinct from a style, is so rare in the modern theatre that, when one encounters it, in Peter Wood's enchanting production, it deserves a loud hurrah . . . There are two performances as good as any I have ever seen in this masterwork. One is the Malaprop of Geraldine McEwan, a comedienne who can raise a laugh with an angry pursing of the lips, a discomforted glare or a fretful twitch of a shoulder . . . The other outstanding performance is a Sir Anthony Absolute to whose testy self-will Michael Hordern brings the autumnal melancholy of the one-time philanderer's "I would if I could".❞
Francis King (Sunday Telegraph)

❝Black and white crescents turn into black and white drawing-rooms and coffee houses, incidentally marking out a semi-circular acting area that is spacious but comfortable. Robert Bryan's lighting takes us meticulously through the single day of the play's action, and lays on a particularly ravishing sunset. Peter Wood directs with his usual accumulation of wit, clarity and showmanship; also with the modicum of restructuring and rewriting he usually affords to old comedies; Mrs Malaprop being allowed ("ah, Sir Anthony, men are all Bavarians") a final malapropism.❞
Robert Cushman (Observer)

All the plays that opened in 1983:

A MAP OF THE WORLD by David Hare, Dir. David Hare, Lyttelton 27.1.83
KICK FOR TOUCH by Peter Gill, Dir. Peter Gill, Cottesloe 15.2.83

SMALL CHANGE by Peter Gill, Dir. Peter Gill, Cottesloe 23.2.83
LORENZACCIO by Alfred de Musset, trans. and adapted by John Fowles, Dir. Michael Bogdanov, Olivier 15.3.83

THE RIVALS by Richard Brinsley Sheridan, Dir. Peter Wood, Olivier 12.4.83
THE TROJAN WAR WILL NOT TAKE PLACE by Jean Giraudoux, English version by Christopher Fry, Dir. Harold Pinter, Lyttelton 10.5.83

Michael Gambon (Ödön von Horváth), **Ian McDiarmid** (Bertolt Brecht)

Donald Cooper

❝I wanted to do a play about Heinrich Mann, but I also wanted to write about Brecht and to say something autobiographical about my own time in California. ❞ *Christopher Hampton*

❝Horváth (in Michael Gambon's superb creation of the character) is a mordant, hedonistic fatalist moving through a society of artists who just happen to represent every conceivable facet of creativity: the establishment figure of Thomas Mann, cagey, stuffy, eminently eminent; Brecht, the social revolutionary, scathing and intolerant while puffing on imported cigars and using his money from the hated movie moguls to invest in another Buick; and the tortured, ageing figure of Thomas's brother Heinrich, the creator of the Blue Angel – starving, prophetically pure in his opposition to the Nazis and unable to prevent his blousy, alcoholic wife from dying. ❞ *Steve Grant (Time Out)*

❝Christopher Hampton has blended the irony and the tragedy of these awkward victims of the times with great skill. With wit and charity he has evoked a period that is sad, shaming, and comic . . . Peter Gill's direction manages to weave together the mixture of realism and symbolism that the author demands. He has also succeeded in turning tragedy into a heart-warming, gripping, and at times very funny experience. ❞ *Milton Shulman (Evening Standard)*

Above: **Billie Whitelaw** (Nelly Mann)

CAST: Michael Gambon *(Ödön von Horváth),* Michael Mueller *(Young Man),* Franc Morgan *(Johnny Weissmuller),* Guy Rolfe *(Thomas Mann),* Roderick Smith *(Chico Marx),* Harry Dickman *(Harpo Marx),* Sylvia Rotter *(Greta Garbo),* John Bluthal *(Charles Money),* Philip Locke *(Heinrich Mann),* Billie Whitelaw *(Nelly Mann),* Pamela Buchner *(Salka Viertel),* Brian Kent *(Walter),* Harry Perscy *(Lion Feuchtwanger),* Mary Chester *(Toni Spuhler),* Sylvia Barter *(Katja Mann),* Barbara Flynn *(Helen Schwartz),* Ian McDiarmid *(Bertolt Brecht),* Sylvia Rotter *(Helene Schwartz),* Paul Imbusch *(Hal),* Belinda Lang *(Angel),* John Bluthal *(Jacob Lomakhin),* Paul Stewart *(Robert E Stripling),* David Baron *(Art Nicely)* With: Eve Adam, Audrey Noble *Musicians:* John White, Timothy Caister, John Harrod, Graham Russell, Roderick Skeaping, Roy Babbington, Helen Tunstall *Directed by* Peter Gill, *Designs by* Alison Chitty, *Lighting by* Stephen Wentworth, *Music by* Terry Davies

1983 TALES FROM HOLLYWOOD
by Christopher Hampton

CAST: Derek Newark *(Shelly Levene),* Karl Johnson *(John Williamson),* Trevor Ray *(Dave Moss),* James Grant *(George Aaronow),* Jack Shepherd *(Richard Roma),* Tony Haygarth *(James Lingk),* John Tams *(Baylen)*
Directed by Bill Bryden, *Designs by* Hayden Griffin, *Lighting by* Andy Phillips

1983 GLENGARRY GLEN ROSS
by David Mamet

Nobby Clark

Jack Shepherd (Richard Roma), **Tony Haygarth** (James Lingk)

❝I wanted to write a play about my time in a real-estate office – it was much wilder than in the play – and that's what it's about.❞
David Mamet

❝The play is filled with the spiralling obscenity and comic bluster of real-estate salesmen caught off-guard; yet underneath that there is fear and desperation. Mamet says that he admires his characters' pragmatic individualism, but to me the piece comes across as a chillingly funny indictment of a world in which you are what you sell.❞
Michael Billington (Guardian)

❝There is a glib, breathtaking momentum in the speech rhythms that Mamet has devised for this pathetic flotsam of the capitalist system. As they talk of the deals and leads and contracts, their conversation is charged with the resentment, anger and frustration of failure. Exhilarated when they close a deal, they are up to every shady trick to prevent a dissatisfied customer from going back on a bargain. Their morality is that of the dollar jungle. The cast superbly handles the expletives, the jargon, the cross-talk of men conspiring and competing with each other as they grasp for a floating prospect like drowning men.❞
Milton Shulman (Evening Standard)

❝A magnificently hard-edged production from Bill Bryden and at just over 1½ hours an evening which operates on all four cylinders.❞
Steve Grant (Time Out)

JEAN SEBERG composer Marvin Hamlisch, lyricist Christopher Adler, dramatist Julian Barry, Dir. Peter Hall, Olivier 1.12.83
CINDERELLA adapted by Bill Bryden, Trevor Ray and the Company, Dir. Bill Bryden, Lyttelton 15.12.83

1984 ANIMAL FARM
by **George Orwell**,
adapted by **Peter Hall**

CAST: Geoffrey Burridge (*Boxer/A Farmer*), Kate Dyson (*The Cat/Napoleon's Dog/A Hen/Pigeons*), Miranda Foster (*Mollie/Napoleon's Dog/A Hen*), Jenny Galloway (*A Hen/A Cow/Mrs Jones/A Pig*), Kamlesh Gupta or Christopher Howard (*The Child*), Greg Hicks (*Snowball/Mr Whymper*), Paul Imbusch (*Mr Jones/The Goose*), Kenny Ireland (*Old Major/Mr Pilkington/A Sheep*), Bill Moody (*A Sheep/A Farmer*), Wendy Morgan (*Minimus/A Hen*), Judith Paris (*Muriel*), Barrie Rutter (*Napoleon*), David Ryall (*Squealer*), Dinah Stabb (*Clover*), Paul Stewart (*Moses/A Hen/Pigeons/A Farmer*), Bev Willis (*Benjamin*)
Musicians: Matthew Scott, Howard Evans, Andrew Findon, John Harrod, Kevin Morgan
Directed by Peter Hall, *Settings, costumes and masks by* Jennifer Carey, *Lighting by* John Bury, *Movement and Assistant Director* Stuart Hopps, *Music Director* Matthew Scott

Left: **Barrie Rutter** (Napoleon)

Nobby Clark

❝The mutinous hens defiantly hurl their eggs down from the Cottesloe balcony until hens' bodies plummet from the flies in cruel reprisal. Animals confessing to treason are dragged off into the barn to amplified screams to leave a final chilling image of blood mingled with snow. And best of all is the moment when the surviving livestock enter on two legs in a tottering, squawking, preening, vile imitation of humanity.❞
Michael Billington (Guardian)

❝Barrie Rutter's Napoleon is an original creation of definitive power: a white-faced pseudo-innocent, taking in every event with unblinking eyes, announcing each curtailment of liberty as if giving his subjects a birthday present, and then lifting his voice in the appalling howl that summons his guard dogs to tear into the enemy. Once seen, never forgotten.❞
Irving Wardle (The Times)

❝Hall's animals are clearly people openly engaged in a brilliant imitation of animal behaviour. They do complete justice to Orwell's humour: they tease your credulity but they never make the mistake of challenging it naturalistically. Jennifer Carey's costumes and masks are cunningly evocative: this is both a fairy story and an animal fable acted by people for people.❞
John Peter (Sunday Times)

❝David Ryall [Squealer] has that shifty flicker in the eyes, that ingratiating sing-song in the voice, that we recognise in all politicians who are either on the make or on the rack.❞
Michael Coveney (Financial Times)

All the plays that opened in 1984:
STRIDER – THE STORY OF A HORSE
by Mark Rozovsky from a story by Tolstoy, in a version by Peter Tegel, Dir. Michael Bogdanov, Cottesloe 26.1.84

SAINT JOAN by Bernard Shaw, Dir. Ronald Eyre. Olivier 16.2.84.
VENICE PRESERV'D by Thomas Otway, Dir. Peter Gill, Lyttelton 12.4.84
ANIMAL FARM by George Orwell, adapted by Peter Hall, Dir. Peter Hall, Cottesloe 25.4.84

ANTIGONE by Sophocles, trans. by C. A. Trypanis, Dir. John Burgess and Peter Gill, Cottesloe 17.5.84
GOLDEN BOY by Clifford Odets, Dir. Bill Bryden, Lyttelton 22.5.84
MANDRAGOLA by Niccolo Machiavelli, translated by Wallace Shawn, Dir. David Gilmore, Olivier 14.6.84

CAST: Karl Johnson *(Dr Triletsky)*, Peter Dineen *(Yakov)*, Kate Gielgud, Annabel Petrie *(Maids)*, Charlotte Cornwell *(Anna Petrovna)*, Basil Henson *(Porfiry Semyonovich Glagolyev)*, Nicholas Jones *(Sergey)*, Brewster Mason *(Colonel Triletzky)*, Elizabeth Garvie *(Sofya)*, Peter Gordon *(Vasily)*, Anthony Douse *(Marko)*, Abigail McKern *(Marya Yefimovna Grekova)*, Ian McKellen *(Platonov)*, Heather Tobias *(Sasha)*, Gertan Klauber *(Gerasim Kuzmich Petrin)*, Roger Lloyd Pack *(Osip)*, Lewis George, Matthew Green *(Peasants)*
Musicians: Dale Culliford, Kevin Leeman, Roderick Skeaping
Director Christopher Morahan, *Settings* John Gunter, *Costumes* Deirdre Clancy, *Music* Dominic Muldowney, *Lighting* Robert Bryan

1984 WILD HONEY
by **Anton Chekhov**, in a version by **Michael Frayn**

Right: **Charlotte Cornwell** (Anna Petrovna), **Ian McKellen** (Platonov)

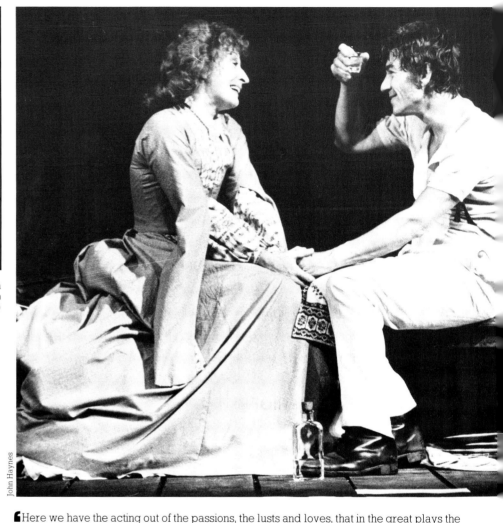

John Haynes

❝Christopher Morahan has given *Wild Honey* a production of extreme confidence and spectacle (when did you last see a man going under a train on stage?) but he has managed also to give it moments of absolute tranquility, so that the final lurch into Feydeau bed-hopping is made all the funnier by its social desperation: "If you won't stay as my wife, stay as my nurse!"❞
Sheridan Morley
(International Herald Tribune)

❝Here we have the acting out of the passions, the lusts and loves, that in the great plays the characters either fail to get to grips with, or only remember or fantasise about. On the one hand, as Sofya, an old flame, says to Platonov: "You keep talking about the past. What does it matter?" On the other: "I don't want my life in front of me, I want it now." And as Platonov says to his wife: "Do you love me?" "Of course I love you." "Why?" asks Ian McKellen's Platonov, and his astonished utterance of the question sends shivers down the spine. Why indeed, unless it is for the glory of Mr McKellen's performance as the playboy of southern Russia, the village schoolmaster, Savonarola Don Juan Platonov.❞
Giles Gordon (Spectator)

ANTON CHEKHOV devised by Michael Pennington, Dir. Michael Pennington, Cottesloe 5.7.84
WILD HONEY by Anton Chekhov, in a version by Michael Frayn, Dir. Christopher Morahan, Lyttelton 19.7.84

A LITTLE HOTEL ON THE SIDE by Georges Feydeau and Maurice Desvallières, trans. by John Mortimer, Dir. Jonathan Lynn, Olivier 9.8.84
FOOL FOR LOVE by Sam Shepard, Dir. Peter Gill, Cottesloe 4.10.84

ROUGH CROSSING by Tom Stoppard, freely adapted from Molnar's *Play at the Castle*, Dir. Peter Wood, Lyttelton 30.10.84
SHE STOOPS TO CONQUER by Oliver Goldsmith, Dir. Giles Block, Lyttelton 8.11.84

John Haynes

CAST: Julie Walters *(May),* Ian Charleson *(Eddie),*
Tom Watson *(The Old Man),* David Troughton
(Martin)
Director Peter Gill, *Designer* Alison Chitty, *Lighting*
Stephen Wentworth

1984 FOOL FOR LOVE
by Sam Shepard

Left: **Julie Walters** (May),
Ian Charleson (Eddie)

❝The man sits at the bare table in the bleak motel room on the edge of the Mojave Desert grinding his fist into the palm of the other hand. The woman droops motionless on the brass bed. He has come back – 2,430 miles he avers – to try again. She knows it is hopeless, wants it not to be, knows it will always be – and anyway what about this "Countess" he has been dating. No good denying it: "I can smell your thoughts before you even think them".❞
Anne Donaldson (Glasgow Herald)

❝Great art can simultaneously traumatise and energise an audience. It is always desired, even by the most humble of witnesses, but it is very rarely delivered. How marvellous then to discover Sam Shepard's astonishing *Fool for Love* . . . It delivers with a vengeance.❞
Ros Asquith (Observer)

❝The play is a metaphysical thriller which feeds on and bitterly mocks the language of the movies and the insecure morality of a nation which was bred on it. For Eddie life, including his own, is a story which has to outdo the greatest myths on celluloid. Peter Gill directs this nightmarish American dream with unremitting tension and Ian Charleson and Julie Walters play with a concentrated ferocity as if every moment were an apocalypse.❞
John Peter (Sunday Times)

THE ANCIENT MARINER, Samuel Taylor Coleridge's
poem adapted by Michael Bogdanov,
Dir. Michael Bogdanov, Olivier 14.11.84
CORIOLANUS by William Shakespeare, Dir. Peter Hall,
Olivier 6.12.84

78

1984

CORIOLANUS
by William Shakespeare

John Haynes

❝McKellen's Coriolanus is a titanic study in arrogance. He's a beautiful animal in war, but in peacetime his body contorts into a neurotic ballet when he must court the favour of the people. His assassination comes not face to face with Roman swords, but at long distance with the stuttering fire of automatic weapons. At the end we hear from the dark a rising roar, the sound of nuclear death.❞ *Jack Kroll (Newsweek)*

❝He is a world-beating athlete, who demands the public's attention and yet resents their praise, lest it should sap his strength (the John McEnroe syndrome perhaps). Caius Martius stands superbly alone, unwilling to change: his pride is the stubbornness of a boy. He is inflexible, incapable of adaptation, like a dinosaur, and the play is the story of his extinction.❞ *Ian McKellen (Acting Shakespeare)*

1985

THE MYSTERIES

from medieval Mystery plays, in a version by the Company with **Tony Harrison**

CAST: Brenda Blethyn or Dinah Stabb *(Mary/Mary Magdalene)*, David Busby *(Morris Dancer/Disciple/Angel)*, Jim Carter *(Mak/Fourth Soldier)*, Edna Doré *(Mrs Noah/Mary Mother)*, Christopher Gilbert *(Wise Man/Simon of Cyrene/Disciple)*, Brian Glover *(God/Cayphas)*, Howard Goorney *(Noah/John the Baptist/Paul)*, James Grant *(Wise Man/Peter)*, Dave Hill *(Joseph/Third Soldier)*, Karl Johnson *(Abel/Jesus)*, Phil Langham *(Disciple/Angel)*, Eve Matheson *(Eve/Mary Salome)*, Derek Newark *(Abraham/Wise Man/First Soldier)*, Robert Oates *(Cain/Barrabas/Disciple)*, Stephen Petcher *(Adam/Isaac/Shepherd/Blind Man/John)*, Trevor Ray *(Shepherd/Second Soldier)*, Jack Shepherd *(Lucifer/Judas/Satan)*, Robert Stephens *(Herod/Pontius Pilate)*, John Tams *(Shepherd/Thomas)*, Anthony Trent *(Herod's son/Annas)*, Don Warrington *(Angel Gabriel)*
The Home Service: Bill Caddick, Jonathan Davie, Howard Evans, Michael Gregory, Stephen King, Graeme Taylor, Roger Williams, Andrew Findon, Phil Langham, Philip Pickett, Linda Thompson
Director Bill Bryden, *Designer* William Dudley, *Lighting* William Dudley and Laurence Clayton, *Music Director* John Tams, *Music arranged and performed by* The Home Service, *Dances arranged by* David Busby

The Nativity: **Dave Hill** (Joseph), **Brenda Blethyn** (Mary)

Nobby Clark

❝The language of the verse is rich with alliteration, bright with colour, wonderfully real with its directness . . . There is not a line anywhere to suggest that the original poet had momentarily forgotten the nature of his audience, or that the adapter has forgotten the nature of his. Again and again, the simplest tricks of staging open an entire realm of effect, so natural is their conception, and this naturalness is the tone of the whole thing . . .

In the uncanonical story of Mak the bad shepherd, Mak is caught stealing sheep, and is sentenced to the pillory. The pillory is one of those seaside joke-photograph devices; the actor puts his head through a hole; and the children in the audience (there are many of them) are invited to pelt him with wet sponges. Many of them enter into the game with zest, but one or two hang back. "Come on", says Mak encouraging them; then he mutters "You won't get a chance like this at *Coriolanus* I can tell you."

It is this welding of actor, audience, play and story into one whole that gives the performance its unique quality – and I wish there were another word for performance, for it diminishes the thing that has been created, which far transcends any idea of a theatre as a place which we visit to see a play, and of a play as that which we visit a theatre to see.❞
Bernard Levin (The Times)

All the plays that opened in 1985:

DOOMSDAY, presented with *The Nativity* and *The Passion* under the generic title of THE MYSTERIES, from medieval mystery plays, version by the Company with Tony Harrison, Dir. Bill Bryden, Cottesloe 19.1.85

THE GOVERNMENT INSPECTOR by Nikolai Gogol in a new version by Adrian Mitchell, Dir. Richard Eyre, Olivier 31.1.85
THE ROAD TO MECCA by Athol Fugard, Dir. Athol Fugard, Lyttelton 27.2.85

MARTINE by Jean-Jacques Bernard, trans. by John Fowles, Dir. Peter Hall, Lyttelton 20.4.85
PRAVDA by Howard Brenton and David Hare, Dir. David Hare, Olivier 2.5.85
THE DUCHESS OF MALFI by John Webster, Dir. Philip Prowse, Lyttelton 4.7.85

❝The relationship of newspapers to this government is like the relationship of *Pravda* to the Soviet government; hence the title. If you came from outside – from Mars, say – and read the British press, you'd think "Oh, they have a lot of government newspapers".❞
David Hare

❝*Pravda* is not merely about a Fleet Street in which the clenched fists of independence have slackened into the limp shrug of the balanced view; it honours a rich tradition of monster-theatre in which Lucifer is super-stitiously believed to have been reborn; the resistible rise of Lambert Le Roux is a parody of the Second Coming.❞
Michael Ratcliffe (Observer)

❝*Pravda* (a kaleidoscopic cartoon look at the "Street of Shame" and a hugely enjoyable satire ranking alongside Jonson's *Volpone*) is the funniest play in London. In South African newspaper proprietor Lambert Le Roux (Anthony Hopkins gives the performance of a lifetime, scuttling about like a wily cockroach and squeezing malicious pleasure from every Afrikaans vowel) Brenton and Hare have created a monstrous monument to the single-minded greed that besets our age.❞
Lyn Gardner (City Limits)

Anthony Hopkins
(Lambert Le Roux)

Nobby Clark

❝Whatever real-world parallels the playwrights may have had in mind for this shrewd, calculatedly savage entrepreneur, Le Roux has a life of his own, and on the grand scale. In Anthony Hopkins' brilliant, buoyant realisation, he is a comic creation as monstrously beguiling as Tartuffe. He shares with Moliere's sham holy man the gift of ever-renewed plausibility.❞
William A. Henry III (Time)

1985

PRAVDA
by **Howard Brenton** and **David Hare**

CAST: Tim McInnerny *(Andrew May)*, Kate Buffery *(Rebecca Foley)*, Ron Pember *(Harry Morrison)*, Fred Pearson *(Hamish McLennan)*, Richard Hope *(Bill Smiley)*, Patricia Franklin *(Moira Patterson)*, Ivor Roberts *(Sir Stamford Foley)*, Ian Bartholomew *(Miles Foley)*, Miranda Foster *(Suzie Fontaine)*, Anthony Hopkins *(Lambert Le Roux)*, Zoë Rutland *(Donna Le Roux)*, Peter Blythe *(Michael Quince)*, Bill Nighy *(Eaton Sylvester)*, Christopher Baines *(D P P Payne)*, Basil Henson *(Elliot Fruit-Norton)*, Norman Warwick *(Waiter)*, Daniel Thorndike *(Bishop of Putney)*, Olivier Pierre *(Lord Silk)*, Guy Williams *(Cliveden Whicker-Baskett)*, Ian Bartholomew *(Mac 'Whipper' Wellington)*, Ian Bartholomew *(Doug Fantom)*, Mark Jax *(Larry Punt)*, Bill Moody *(Jack 'Breaker' Bond)*, Nigel le Vaillant *(Leander Scroop)*, William Sleigh *(Cartoonist)*, Harriet Thorpe *(Princess Jill)*, Jenny Galloway *(Barmaid)*, Olivier Pierre *(Ian Ape-Warden)*, Fred Pearson *(Hannon Spot)*, Desmond Adams *(Photographer)*, Robert Ralph, Paul Stewart *(Journalists)*, Glenn Williams *(Newsvendor)*
Director David Hare, *Settings* Hayden Griffin, *Costumes* Lindy Hemming, *Music* Nick Bicât

A CHORUS OF DISAPPROVAL by Alan Ayckbourn, Dir. Alan Ayckbourn, Olivier 1.8.85
THE REAL INSPECTOR HOUND by Tom Stoppard, Dir. Tom Stoppard, and THE CRITIC by Richard Brinsley Sheridan, Dir. Sheila Hancock, Olivier 12.9.85

FESTIVAL OF NEW PLAYS:
THE MURDERERS by Daniel Mornin, Dir. Peter Gill, Cottesloe 23.9.85;
TRUE DARE KISS by Debbie Horsfield, Dir. John Burgess, Cottesloe 3.10.85;

AS I LAY DYING by Peter Gill from William Faulkner, Dir. Peter Gill, Cottesloe 15.10.85;
COMMAND OR PROMISE by Debbie Horsfield, Dir. John Burgess, Cottesloe 24.10.85;

Bob Peck (Guy Jones), **Michael Gambon** (Dafydd Ap Llewellyn), **Imelda Staunton** (Hannah Llewellyn)

Nobby Clark

❛Instead of having a central character who is a dynamo driving everyone on, I've always been interested in having a vacuum, a giant slate that everyone scribbles on. I'm interested in people who aren't in control of their career. I've never been in control of mine.❜
Alan Ayckbourn

❛The pairing of Peck and Gambon is dream casting and pays expected dividends. There are, too, any number of cameos and small observations to savour: the pianist in his mac and pork-pie hat; the sour, local burgher, obsessed with the mistaken idea that Jones is Scottish; the self-important post-rehearsal banter in the pub.❜
Jim Hiley (Listener)

❛Ayckbourn . . . belongs to the comic tradition of Jonson and Moliere, but with the important difference that he's entirely free of preachifying, and even his most vitriolic observations are tinged with the wry and spontaneous sympathy of a fellow creature.❜
John Peter (Sunday Times)

❛The story, which could not have been told more entertainingly, raises interesting moral questions. Guy is not evil, malicious or calculating. He is not even particularly greedy or lascivious, but he is unable to say no when an attractive married lady offers herself. . . As he gets drawn into situations which cause suffering, confusion and consternation, the play picks up on the satirical content of *The Beggar's Opera*.❜
Ronald Hayman (Plays International)

1985 A CHORUS OF DISAPPROVAL
by Alan Ayckbourn

CAST: Bob Peck *(Guy Jones)*, Michael Gambon *(Dafydd Ap Llewellyn)*, Imelda Staunton *(Hannah Llewellyn)*, Jenny Galloway *(Bridget Baines)*, Paul Todd *(Mr Ames)*, Jane Wenham *(Enid Washbrook)*, Moira Redmond *(Rebecca Huntley-Pike)*, Gemma Craven *(Fay Hubbard)*, Paul Bentall *(Ian Hubbard)*, David Ryall *(Jarvis Huntley-Pike)*, James Hayes *(Ted Washbrook)*, Daniel Flynn *(Crispin Usher)*, Kelly Hunter *(Linda Washbrook)*, Michael Beint *(Reginald Bickerdyke)*, Mary Chester *(Georgina Coombes)*, Kate Dyson *(Monica Bickerdyke)*, Virginia Greig *(Sharon Fitch)*, Robert Ralph *(Raymond Finegan)*, Simon Scott *(Tony Mofitt)*, Janet Whiteside *(Annie Anderson)*
Director Alan Ayckbourn, *Settings* Alan Tagg, *Costumes* Lindy Hemming, *Lighting* Mick Hughes, *Music Director* Paul Todd, *Dances* Olivia Breeze

---

FIVE PLAY BILL: A Twist of Lemon by Alex Renton, Dir. Peter Gill; *Sunday Morning* by Rod Smith, Dir. John Burgess; *In The Blue* by Peter Gill, Dir. Peter Gill; *Bouncing* by Rosemary Wilton, Dir. Peter Gill; *Up for None* by Mick Mahoney, Dir. Peter Gill, Cottesloe 6.11.85;

THE GARDEN OF ENGLAND edited by Peter Cox and the Company, Dir. John Burgess and Peter Gill, Cottesloe 14.11.85
MRS WARREN'S PROFESSION by Bernard Shaw, Dir. Anthony Page, Lyttelton 10.10.85

LOVE FOR LOVE by William Congreve, Dir. Peter Wood, Lyttelton 13.11.85
YONADAB by Peter Shaffer, Dir. Peter Hall, Olivier 4.12.85
THE CHERRY ORCHARD by Anton Chekhov, trans. by Mike Alfreds with Lilia Sokolov, Dir. Mike Alfreds, Cottesloe 10.12.85

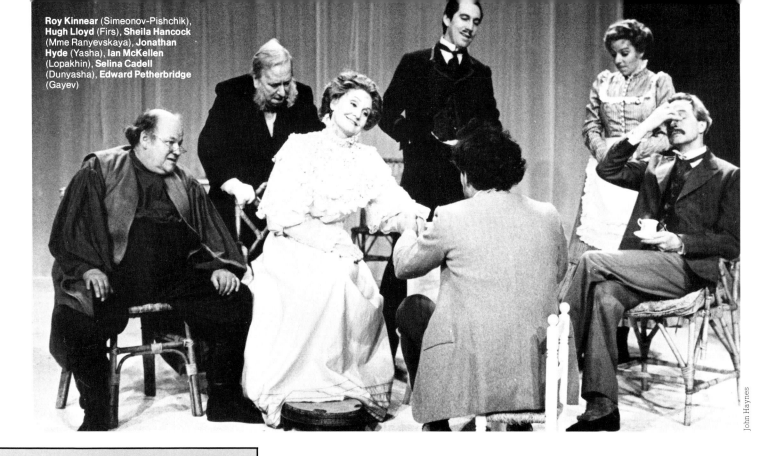

Roy Kinnear (Simeonov-Pishchik), **Hugh Lloyd** (Firs), **Sheila Hancock** (Mme Ranyevskaya), **Jonathan Hyde** (Yasha), **Ian McKellen** (Lopakhin), **Selina Cadell** (Dunyasha), Edward Petherbridge (Gayev)

John Haynes

1985

THE CHERRY ORCHARD
by **Anton Chekhov**,
trans. by **Mike Alfreds**
with **Lilia Sokolov**

CAST: Selina Cadell *(Dunyasha),* Ian McKellen *(Lopakhin),* Greg Hicks *(Yepikhodov),* Hugh Lloyd *(Firs),* Claire Moore *(Anya),* Sheila Hancock *(Ranyevskaya),* Eleanor Bron *(Varya),* Edward Petherbridge *(Gayev),* Julie Legrand *(Charlotta Ivanovna),* Roy Kinnear *(Simeonov-Pishchik),* Jonathan Hyde *(Yasha),* Laurance Rudic *(Trofimov),* Peter Needham *(a passer-by),* Simon Dutton *(the station master),* Tristram Wymark *(the post office clerk)*
Musicians: Rory Allam, Roy Babbington, Nicholas Hayley
Director Mike Alfreds, *Design and Lighting* Paul Dart, *Music* Ilona Sekacz, *Dances* Sue Lefton

❝When I walked down to the stage with Edward he *was* my brother, Gayev, and when I ran on to the stage it *was* "my darling nursery". There was one wavering moment when I looked out at the orchard and caught sight of the impassive face of one of the critics but, whereas normally my mind would have been distracted, somehow it jumped back into the play. It was a miracle. All those groundless, destructive fears of previous first nights seemed to have dissolved. I actually enjoyed myself.❞
Sheila Hancock (Ramblings of an Actress)

❝Never in any British Chekhov I've seen have the characters listened to each other less; never has the dilemma of each been shown with more immediacy.❞
Jim Hiley (Listener)

❝If the play is about change and resistance to change, Chekhov also shows connection with the past as something precious in itself, a part of each character's identity. Characters come strangely alive in Chekhov, but so does the greater historical moment, as power begins to transfer from the ruling class to the peasant. Mike Alfreds' production is breathtakingly good. It is fine, subtle, comic and extremely sad. He has cast and directed so well that each character looks mysteriously as if he or she had the quintessential face for that part.❞
Kathy O'Shaughnessy (Spectator)

John Haynes

1986 BRIGHTON BEACH MEMOIRS
by Neil Simon

CAST: Steven Mackintosh *(Eugene Jerome),* Alison Fiske *(Blanche Morton),* Frances de la Tour *(Kate Jerome),* Belinda Buckley *(Laurie Morton),* Lisa Jacobs *(Nora Morton),* Robert Glenister *(Stanley Jerome),* Harry Towb *(Jack Jerome)*
Director Michael Rudman, *Settings* Carl Toms, *Costumes* Lindy Hemming, *Lighting* Leonard Tucker

Steven Mackintosh (Eugene Jerome)

❝*Brighton Beach Memoirs* comes out of O'Neill and Odets and perhaps above all, Arthur Miller's *Death of a Salesman*. Here, too, we have a father facing unemployment in the late 1930s; here, too, we have two sons in love, and at war with each other; here, too we have a mother holding a family together because that is the only way she can hold herself together. Sure, Simon inclines to comedy where Miller inclined his family to tragedy; but in his own memory of himself at fifteen, Simon has come up with a touching and marvellous narrator.❞
Sheridan Morley *(Punch)*

❝American plus Jewish sentimentality might have drenched us with two separate buckets of slush – but Simon's sombre moments always have a poignant truth. And he has the marvellous gift of being able to dispel gloom instantly – not with wisecracking one-liners, but with a humour that raises spirits as well as laughs.❞
Kenneth Hurren *(Mail on Sunday)*

❝Michael Rudman's splendidly paced production gives us age-gaps, adolescent longings, the importantance of trivia to human and familial relationships, the need for independence and the ties of the familiar, all set against a world backdrop that creeps slowly nearer to the porch . . . Simon's most mature and thoughtful piece.❞
Steve Grant *(Time Out)*

All the plays that opened in 1986:

HAMLET by William Shakespeare, Dir. Cicely Berry, Cottesloe 9.1.86 (NT Education presentation)
NOT ABOUT HEROES by Stephen MacDonald, Dir. Michael Simpson, Cottesloe 13.2.86

BRIGHTON BEACH MEMOIRS by Neil Simon, Dir. Michael Rudman, Lyttelton 25.2.86
THE THREEPENNY OPERA by Bertolt Brecht and Kurt Weill, trans. by Robert David MacDonald, Dir. Peter Wood, Olivier 13.3.86

FUTURISTS by Dusty Hughes, Dir. Richard Eyre, Cottesloe 17.3.86
DALLIANCE Arthur Schnitzler's *Liebelei* in a version by Tom Stoppard, Dir. Peter Wood, Lyttelton 27.5.86
NEAPTIDE by Sarah Daniels, Dir. John Burgess, Cottesloe 2.7.86

Nobby Clark

Above: **Deborah Leighton** (Cosima Beamer), **Sarah Prince** (Arianalla Skiller), **John Darrell** (Dr Mungadory), **Nicola Blackman** (Lady Lucy Saveloy), **Elaine Lordan** (Bobby "Gravy" Browning), **Sylvester McCoy** (Pied Piper), **Shaun Curry** (Baron Saveloy), **Richard O'Callaghan** (Boko Bandy), **Graham Sinclair** (Boggle), **Sammy Johnson** (Goggle)

1986

THE PIED PIPER
by **Adrian Mitchell**,
devised by **Alan Cohen**,
music by
Dominic Muldowney,
from **Robert Browning**

CAST: Deborah Leighton *(Cosima Beamer),* John Darrell *(Dr Mungadory),* Sarah Prince *(Arianalla Skiller),* Mike Hayward *(Nutter Mausenheimer),* Yvonne Gidden *(Twessa Twangalang),* Richard O'Callaghan *(Boko Bandy),* Graham Sinclair *(Boggle),* Sammy Johnson *(Goggle),* Shaun Curry *(Baron Dennis Saveloy),* Nicola Blackman *(Lady Lucy Saveloy),* Bill Moody *(The Hon. Egbert Saveloy),* Elaine Lordan *(Bobby 'Gravy' Browning),* Wendy Morgan *(Toffee Jenkins),* Richard Platt *(King Rat),* Sylvester McCoy *(The Pied Piper),* Deborah Leighton, Elaine Lordan, Sarah Prince *(The Rodents),* Mike Hayward *(The Rampant Umbrage),* Deborah Leighton *(The Iced Knight),* Tasha *(Coffee),* and the children from thirteen ILEA primary schools *(The Massed Rats)*
Musicians: Robert Lockhart, Anthony Aldridge, Julia Findon, Michael Gregory, David Roach, David Stewart
Director Alan Cohen, *Settings* Roger Glossop, *Costumes* Sally Gardner, *Company movement* Jane Gibson, *Lighting* Paul McLeish

❛Mitchell's Piper is set in a funky Hamelin (superb sets by Roger Glossop) besieged by rocker rats in leather gear boogying to Dominic Muldowney's pop-style music. Mitchell suffuses the tale which has thrilled and chilled children for generations, with the idea of adult greed versus love and childhood innocence.❜
Ann McFerran (Time Out)

❛Both the rats and the kids are played, with tremendous professionalism and verve, by children from 13 inner-London primary schools. In rodent guise they jive and scratch with an enthusiasm which only a combination of an Elvis Presley-rat and the thought of all that luncheon could inspire. In the second half, after the Piper has taken his revenge on the perfidious mayor, the crowded junk of Hamelin recedes and luminous magical stage effects accompany the children and their leader on their quest to the fairytale mountain.❜
Harry Eyres (The Times)

❛McCoy is a superb children's actor, likeable but grave, quaint but reassuring, soft-voiced but driven by a spry and sinister energy. Dressed in a frock coat of kaleidoscopic patchwork, with striped trousers and braces, he is half old-fashioned street-busker and half eerie hobgoblin. It is never difficult to believe in the fickle world of faerie from which he comes.❜
Andrew Rissik (The Independent)

JACOBOWSKY AND THE COLONEL original play by Franz Werfel, English-language version by S. N. Behrman, Dir. Jonathan Lynn, Olivier 22.7.86
THE PETITION by Brian Clark, Dir. Peter Hall, Lyttelton 30.7.86

THE AMERICAN CLOCK by Arthur Miller, Dir. Peter Wood, Cottesloe 6.8.86
THE BAY AT NICE and WRECKED EGGS by David Hare, Dir. David Hare, Cottesloe 9.9.86
THE MAGISTRATE by Arthur W. Pinero, Dir. Michael Rudman, Lyttelton 24.9.86

TONS OF MONEY by Will Evans and Valentine, Dir. Alan Ayckbourn, Lyttelton 6.11.86
THE PIED PIPER by Adrian Mitchell from Robert Browning, Devised and Dir. by Alan Cohen, Music Dominic Muldowney, Olivier 11.11.86

Anthony Hopkins (Lear)

Nobby Clark

Anthony Hopkins (Lear),
Michael Bryant (Gloucester)

Nobby Clark

❝The story works its own fascination. Children love it. They don't know why, but there's something about a madman playing near a beach with a blind man which rivets their attention . . . But over and above that it's like *Hamlet* – it has to be reinvented and it will always reflect the age. People always temperamentally prefer one play or the other. I'm a Lear-ist.❞
David Hare (NT's programme)

❝What is so splendid about Hare's production is that it has a consistency of vision which never shirks the play's bleakness. There is no comfort to be found in it, no suggestion that the old state of muddled order is to be restored. The characters who remain alive at the end must make shift as best they can, in a world whose innocence has been stripped away by a fully realised vision of horror.❞
Joan Smith (Today)

❝No one else can mobilise the stage as Hopkins can, generating physically the emotional turbulence and paradox which lie at the centre of a character. In *King Lear* his rages were wrestling matches with a hostile universe; and at the end, he was not crushed by suffering but dazed and stupefied by it, his mind seemingly separated from the material world by the pell-mell violence continually done to him.❞
Andrew Rissik (Plays International)

CAST: Philip Locke *(Kent)*, Michael Bryant *(Gloucester)*, Douglas Hodge *(Edmund)*, Anthony Hopkins *(Lear)*, Anna Massey *(Goneril)*, Miranda Foster *(Cordelia)*, Suzanne Bertish *(Regan)*, Ken Drury *(Albany)*, Fred Pearson *(Cornwall)*, Guy Williams *(Burgundy)*, Philip Brook *(King of France)*, Bill Nighy *(Edgar)*, Basil Henson *(Oswald)*, Brian Spink *(Knight)*, Roshan Seth *(Fool)*, Desmond Adams *(Gentleman)*, Martin Bax *(Curan)*, Peter Gordon *(First Servant)*, Simon Needs *(Second Servant)*, Peter Attard *(Third Servant)*, Daniel Thorndike *(Old Man)*, Hus Levent *(Messenger)*, Daniel Thorndike *(Doctor)*, Glenn Williams *(Bedlam beggar)*, Ian Bolt, Patrick Brennan *(French soldiers)*, Judith Coke, Helen Fitzgerald, Janet Whiteside *(Ladies)*
Musicians: Terry Davies, Paul Higgs, Stephen King, Anthony Wagstaff, George Weigand, John Wilbraham
Director David Hare, *Settings* Hayden Griffin, *Costumes* Christine Stromberg, *Lighting* Rory Dempster, *Music* Nick Bicât, *Fights arranged by* Terry King

1986

KING LEAR
by **William Shakespeare**

KING LEAR by William Shakespeare, Dir. David Hare, Olivier 11.12.86
THE MOTHER by Bertolt Brecht, Dir. Di Trevis, Cottesloe 11.12.86 (NT Education presentation)

1987

A VIEW FROM THE BRIDGE
by Arthur Miller

CAST: Michael Gambon *(Eddie Carbone),* Elizabeth Bell *(Beatrice),* Suzan Sylvester *(Catherine),* James Hayes *(Alfieri),* Michael Simkins *(Marco),* Adrian Rawlins *(Rodolpho),* Russell Dixon *(Louis),* John Arthur *(Mike),* Paul Todd *(Tony),* Allan Mitchell *(First immigration officer),* Simon Coady *(Second immigration officer),* Lewis George *(Mr Lipari),* Mary Chester *(Mrs Lipari),* Kate Dyson *(Submarine woman),* Paul Todd *(Submarine man)*
Director Alan Ayckbourn, *Settings* Alan Tagg, *Costumes* Lindy Hemming, *Lighting* Mick Hughes, *Dialect Coach* Joan Washington

❝This mighty production fills the Cottesloe with far more than distant echoes of a dark age. And to imply that it is merely a play about incest and hints of homosexuality is to say that *Macbeth* is about dinner parties and fortune telling. Ayckbourn's imperceptible hand points it up as a classic for all times.❞ *Jack Tinker (Daily Mail)*

❝Mr Gambon's stocky build is fleet of foot and light of movement. He charts Eddie's growing, if unrealised, jealousy of the handsome illegal immigrant sheltered in his home, from narrowed eyes as the boy exuberantly bursts into song to an uncharacteristically angry comment on Catherine's new high heels. Thereafter he knows no peace: "A passion had moved into his body like a stranger."❞ *Martin Hoyle (Financial Times)*

❝The big hero is the star, Michael Gambon, who as the sexually confused Brooklyn longshoreman not only gets the accent right but also the character's tensions, pretensions and blustering coarseness in what adds up to a portrayal as convincing as it is compelling.❞ *Jack Pitman (Variety)*

❝It is not even enough to declare that there is not an English actor alive who could do it as well, let alone better. To Gambon belongs the ultimate accolade . . . he *is* Eddie Carbone.❞ *Robin Ray (Punch)*

Nobby Clark

Michael Gambon (Eddie Carbone)

All the plays that opened in 1987:

COMING IN TO LAND by Stephen Poliakoff, Dir. Peter Hall, Lyttelton 7.1.87
THREE MEN ON A HORSE by George Abbott and John Cecil Holm, Dir. Jonathan Lynn, Cottesloe 22.1.87

SCHOOL FOR WIVES by Molière, trans. by Robert David MacDonald, Dir. Di Trevis, Lyttelton 29.1.87
A VIEW FROM THE BRIDGE by Arthur Miller, Dir. Alan Ayckbourn, Cottesloe 12.2.87

SIX CHARACTERS IN SEARCH OF AN AUTHOR by Luigi Pirandello, version by Nicholas Wright, Dir. Michael Rudman, Olivier 18.3.87
YERMA by Federico Garcia Lorca, trans. by Peter Luke, Dir. Di Trevis, Cottesloe 26.3.87

Anthony Hopkins (Antony),
Judi Dench (Cleopatra)

John Haynes

❝The narrative sweep and dramatic tension Peter Hall brings to the sprawling text carries the audience along on a swell of invention and high theatricality that never lets up. And, praise be! it is meticulously cast, down to the lowliest spear-carrier. As Mark Antony, Anthony Hopkins dominates the proceedings with a memorable study of grizzled nobility gone to seed. Both physically and vocally he is superb. It is a performance whose power and passion is matched by Judi Dench's towering spit-fire Cleopatra. Ms Dench's range is positively awesome. There is no emotion she leaves unexpressed.❞
Clive Hirschhorn (Sunday Express)

❝An excellent company, led by first-rate actors in supporting roles and headed by two players of genius, gives the fullest account of the tragedy I have ever seen. Trusting the text, allowing the verse to exert its magic, Hall paces the action perfectly, clearly distinguishing between Rome's cold virtue and the heady languor of the East.❞
John James
(Times Educational Supplement)

❝British theatre at its spellbinding and magnificent best. This is a big, heroic play in every sense, and Hall's control over it is complete. The huge spans of the action tense up, arch and unfold like great symphonic movements, and the poetry of this sensuous athletic text tolls with burnished conviction.❞
John Peter (Sunday Times)

CAST: Anthony Hopkins *(Mark Antony),* Tim Pigott-Smith *(Octavius),* John Bluthal *(Lepidus),* Michael Bryant *(Domitius Enobarbus),* Mike Hayward *(Philo),* Jeremy Flynn *(Eros),* Brian Spink *(Ventidius),* Andrew C Wadsworth *(Scarus),* Daniel Thorndike *(Canidius),* Desmond Adams *(Silius),* Michael Carter *(Decretas),* Sally Dexter *(Octavia),* Basil Henson *(Agrippa),* Brian Spink *(Demetrius),* Graham Sinclair *(Maecenas),* Desmond Adams *(Thidias),* Andrew C Wadsworth *(Dolabella),* Brian Spink *(Proculeius),* Desmond Adams *(Gallus),* Frances Quinn *(Lady attending on Octavia),* David Schofield *(Sextus Pompey),* Peter Gordon *(Menecrates),* Michael Carter *(Menas),* Michael Bottle *(Varrius),* Peter Corey/Paul Vinhas *(Boy),* Judi Dench *(Cleopatra),* Miranda Foster *(Charmian),* Helen Fitzgerald *(Iras),* Robert Arnold *(Alexas),* John Bluthal *(Clown),* Iain Ormsby-Knox *(Mardian),* Robert Arnold *(Diomedes),* Daniel Thorndike *(Seleucus),* Peter Gordon *(Schoolmaster),* Daniel Thorndike *(Soothsayer),* Michael Bottle *(Egyptian)* Ian Bolt, Patrick Brennan, Hus Levent, Simon Needs, Simon Scott *(Messengers and Soldiers)* *Musicians:* Michael Brain, Michael Gregory, Howard Hawkes, Colin Rae, Roderick Skeaping, Nicholas Hayley, David Tosh, George Weigand.
Director Peter Hall, *Designer* Alison Chitty, *Lighting* Stephen Wentworth, *Music* Dominic Muldowney

1987 ANTONY AND CLEOPATRA
by **William Shakespeare**

Nobby Clark

Michael Gambon (Jack McCracken), **Polly Adams** (Poppy McCracken), **Suzan Sylvester** (Samantha McCracken), *in bath* **Simon Cadell** (Benedict Hough), **Diane Bull** (Tina Ruston)

1987 A SMALL FAMILY BUSINESS
by Alan Ayckbourn

CAST: Michael Gambon *(Jack McCracken),* Polly Adams *(Poppy),* Ron Pember *(Ken Ayres),* Diane Bull *(Tina),* Adrian Rawlins *(Roy Ruston),* Suzan Sylvester *(Samantha),* Russell Dixon *(Cliff),* Elizabeth Bell *(Anita),* John Arthur *(Desmond),* Marcia Warren *(Harriet),* Barbara Hicks *(Yvonne),* Simon Cadell *(Benedict Hough),* Michael Simkins *(the Rivetti Brothers)*
Director Alan Ayckbourn, *Settings* Alan Tagg, *Costumes* Lindy Hemming, *Lighting* Mick Hughes, *Music* Paul Todd

❝If you boil down your themes, they seem terribly banal. But there are still things to say about the fear and dislike people have for each other and the fact that members of each sex are like Martians to the other.❞ *Alan Ayckbourn*

❝Ayckbourn's sizzling, bitter new comedy [is] a morality play depicting a grasping society where goodness is boring and corruption sexy, where possession of a Porsche means more than human relationships and where pinching a paper-clip is one step on the slippery slope to full-scale murder.❞ *Jane Edwardes (Time Out)*

❝The play takes place in a present-day England where commercial greed and the bogus claims of family loyalty have distorted every decent value. Amid the corruption, one man – a typically decent but weak Ayckbourn hero   tries to behave decently, but is dragged relentlessly down in scenes of extraordinary horror.❞
Sean French (New Society)

❝This is a world of hustlers, dodgers, fixers, where anyone managing to have it off with not one but five corrupt Italian businessmen qualifies, as soon as she has completed the set, for a free gallon of petrol. Michael Gambon plays the honest businessman, faithful husband and devoted son-in-law, who needs to be taught a lesson: a massive, latter-day Candide, moving by violent stages from bewilderment, incredulity and stupefaction to relaxed and resplendent villainy.❞
Hilary Spurling (Times Literary Supplement)

ENTERTAINING STRANGERS by David Edgar,
Dir. Peter Hall, Cottesloe 15.10.87
WAITING FOR GODOT by Samuel Beckett,
Dir. Michael Rudman, Lyttelton 25.11.87

COUNTRYMANIA a trilogy by Carlo Goldoni
(*Country Fever, Country Hazards, Country Harvest*)
in a version by Mike Alfreds, Dir. Mike Alfreds,
Olivier 12.12.87

❝I started with an impossible situation and a notebook. It's not a campaigning play, at least not obviously, although a gay love affair is at its centre. It was only when I'd finished it that I realised how much class hatred is in it.❞
Peter Gill (City Limits)

❝*Mean Tears* is a moving, powerful and compulsive portrait of contemporary life. The dialogue reflects the overprivileged need of the characters. Gushing, staccato and freighted with allusion, it tacks to its contradictory conclusion as confused and confusing as they are. The acting is superlatively, hallucinatorily accurate.❞
Simon Burt (Times Literary Supplement)

❝In Gill's meticulous choreography, where distances between actors seem to have been decided to the last millimetre, invisible frontiers sprout up all over that vacant expanse, reflecting the forces of attraction and repulsion. The same process operates in the text which shows characters using words to claim psychological space or take possession of someone else's, either with bursts of arbitrary aggression, abrupt changes of the subject, or declamatory appeals for sympathy.❞
Irving Wardle (The Times)

CAST: Bill Nighy *(Julian)*, Karl Johnson *(Stephen)*, Garry Cooper *(Paul)*, Hilary Dawson *(Celia)*, Emma Piper *(Nell)*
Director Peter Gill, *Designer* Alison Chitty, *Lighting* Stephen Wentworth

89

1987 MEAN TEARS
by Peter Gill

Bill Nighy (Julian),
Karl Johnson (Stephen)

Donald Cooper

'Reworking the play for the National gave me the opportunity to develop the relationships of the central characters, and to deepen the conflict between them. I've also allowed myself greater leeway with the history. It's very different. But it nevertheless remains a true story about actual people, set in a real place more than a hundred years ago.' *David Edgar*

'A richly detailed picture is assembled. Characters are rapidly sketched, narrators pop up from all over the auditorium and we are carried along on a tide of mid 19th-century Dorchester town life. Moule himself, played with complete conviction by Tim Pigott-Smith manages to be both ridiculous and serious – a considerable and subtle achievement by the actor. He is a man of conviction, but he is also a killjoy prig.'
Christopher Edwards *(Spectator)*

'Peter Hall's production is a revelation. The Cottesloe auditorium becomes earth and heaven and hell. At one end, the vicarage; at the other, the alehouse; in between the promenading audience, the actors, the action. The company indeed entertains its strangers, reaching out with the embraces of music and dance, words and emotions. Edgar's story of cholera and compassion is a moving parable for our AIDS-ridden, victim-blaming days: "Be not forgetful to entertain strangers: for thereby some have entertained angels unawares."'
Roy Porter *(Times Literary Supplement)*

Tim Pigott-Smith (Rev Moule), **and promenade audience**

John Haynes

1987 ENTERTAINING STRANGERS
by David Edgar

CAST: Robert Arnold *(Henry Frampton/Alfred Mason/William Fudge/Benjamin Voss)*, John Bluthal *(Capt. William Henning/William Bartlett/Mr Macarte)*, Richard Bonneville *(George Loder/John Lock/ Sergeant)*, Michael Bottle *(John James Besant/ Lt. Vandaleur/George Andrews)*, Patrick Brennan *(George Moule/Thomas Patch/Warder)*, Michael Byrne *(Charles Eldridge/John Floyer)*, Nadia Chambers *(Sarah Albinia Eldridge/Martha Whiting)*, Charlotte Coleman *(Sophie Eldridge/Lizzie Sibley)*, Garry Cooper *(Horace Moule)*, Judi Dench *(Sarah Eldridge)*, Sally Dexter *(Christian/Ann Henning)*, Helen Fitzgerald *(Emily Eldridge/Jane Sibley)*, Jenny Galloway *(Ann Besant/Martha Lock)*, Peter Gordon *(James Brooks/John Galpin)*, Ian Harris *(Charles Moule as a child/Albert Sibley)*, Corin Helliwell *(Charles Eldridge as a child/George Moule as a child)*, Shirley Henderson *(Fanny Lock)*, Basil Henson *(Robert William/Dr Christopher Arden/Natty Seale)*, James Hillier-Brook *(Charles Moule as a child/Albert Sibley)*, Joanne Lamb *(Hannah/Florence Chaffley as a child)*, Steven Mackintosh *(Handley Moule/Edward Fudge/Jimmy)*, Mary Macleod *(Mary Frampton/Jane Whiting)*, Laura McMahon *(Sophie Eldridge as a child/Louisa Lock)*, Tim Pigott-Smith *(Henry Moule)*, Frances Quinn *(Ellen Wright/ Florence Chaffley/Sarah Holland)*, Annabelle Ryan *(Sophie as a child/Louisa Lock)*, Simon Scott *(Charles Moule/Mr Turnley)*, Nicholas Simpson *(Charles Eldridge as a child/George Moule as a child)*, Janet Whiteside *(Mary Moule)*, Peter Woodward *(John Tizard/Capt. Augustus Handley/ Mr Hengler)*
The Mellstock Band: David Townsend, Ian Blake, Mark Emerson, Christopher Wood
Director Peter Hall, *Designer* William Dudley, *Lighting* Gerry Jenkinson, *Music* Dominic Muldowney

Nobby Clark

❝I'm more and more convinced that the play is like one man's dialogue with himself, rather like the two Byzantium poems of Yeats are a dialogue within the poet's head ... I think that this play simply happened in his head and that this is the only possible landscape for it.❞
Michael Rudman (NT's programme)

❝Futile expectation paralyses Vladimir and Estragon: false hope tethers them to the tree where they wait for Godot. Estragon, whose painful feet receive constant mention, can only hobble. Vladimir manoeuvres himself with "short, stiff strides". Taking hold of all this more as a masseur and osteopath than a producer, Rudman loosens the play into something unexpectedly limber. Alec McCowen's Vladimir – a chirpy chap with bright eyes and a healthy pippin-like complexion – bounces lightly on the balls of his plimsolled feet and bounds around the set's artfully disposed ledges and declivities as agilely as a gazelle. Verbally too, he quivers with vitality: vocal jauntiness frequently gives a lift to lines Beckett has laden with glumness. John Alderton's Estragon, bulkier and sulkier, provides a dour foil for his nippy, chipper performance.❞
Peter Kemp (The Independent)

Left: **John Alderton** (Vladimir),
Alec McCowen (Estragon)

1987 WAITING FOR GODOT
by **Samuel Beckett**

CAST: John Alderton *(Estragon),* Alec McCowen *(Vladimir),* Colin Welland *(Pozzo),* Peter Wight *(Lucky),* Simon Privett/Simon Doe *(Boy)*
Director Michael Rudman, *Setting* William Dudley, *Costumes* Lindy Hemming, *Lighting* Robert Bryan

1988

CAT ON A HOT TIN ROOF
by Tennessee Williams

CAST: Lindsay Duncan *(Margaret)*, Ian Charleson *(Brick)*, Alison Steadman *(Mae)*, Barbara Leigh-Hunt *(Big Mama)*, Julie-Ann Forde *(Dixie)*, Eric Porter *(Big Daddy)*, Colin Jeavons *(Rev. Tooker)*, Paul Jesson *(Gooper)*, Henry Goodman *(Dr. Baugh)*, Major Wiley *(Lacey)*, Doreen Ingleton *(Sookey)*, Donald Campbell *(Brightie)*, Margo Selby *(Trixie)*, Emma Kruse *(Polly)*, Darren Weir *(Buster)*, James Ross *(Sonny)*
Director Howard Davies, *Designer* William Dudley, *Lighting* Mark Henderson, *Music composed by* Ilona Sekacz, *Dialect coach* Joan Washington

Right: **Ian Charleson** (Brick),
Lindsay Duncan (Maggie)

John Haynes

❝I meant for the audience to discover how people erect false values by not facing what is true in their natures, by having to live a lie, and I hoped the audience would admire the heroic persistence of life and vitality; and I hoped they would feel the thwarted desire of people to reach each other.❞
Tennessee Williams

❝Almost retching on the word "disgust", choking as his talk brings up the homo-sexuality that so appals him, stuttering near-hysterically as suppressed responses battle for expression against clenched panic, Charleson makes Brick's paralysed predica-ment painfully moving . . . Also tightening the tension in this central scene is Eric Porter's massively impressive Big Daddy – a performance that loses none of the man's redneck crudity while catching every nuance of his irritable wit and almost cynical tolerance.❞
Peter Kemp (The Independent)

❝Howard Davies crosses the river to direct as powerful, poetic and spell-binding a version of this piece as you are likely to see . . . Miss Duncan finds new depth and edge to her comedy playing, a lethal vengefulness breaking around her golden hair and alabaster shoulders. Mr Charleson is stricken almost to the point of catatonia, a ruined athlete in shimmering white exactly conjuring the Williams ideal of a helpless male divinity. These are two performances of driven majesty and great poise.❞
Michael Coveney (Financial Times)

All the plays that opened up to the NT's 25th birthday in 1988:

CAT ON A HOT TIN ROOF by Tennessee Williams, Dir. Howard Davies, Lyttelton 3.2.88

A PLACE WITH THE PIGS by Athol Fugard, Dir. Athol Fugard, Cottesloe 16.2.88
'TIS PITY SHE'S A WHORE by John Ford, Dir. Alan Ayckbourn, Olivier 3.3.88
FANSHEN by David Hare, Dir. Les Waters, Cottesloe 31.3.88 (NT Education presentation)

THE SHAUGHRAUN by Dion Boucicault, Dir. Howard Davies, Olivier 11.5.88
THE WINTER'S TALE, THE TEMPEST and CYMBELINE by William Shakespeare, Dir. Peter Hall, Cottesloe 18.5.88, 19.5.88, 20.5.88 respectively

❝Roll up, roll up, to see the greatest revolving stage on earth! Thrill to the glorious sight of heroes abseiling down the battlements of a ruined abbey! Gnash your dentures with rage at scoundrels taking advantage of damsels in distress! It is difficult to do justice to this splendid National Theatre production of Victorian drama without gushing like Niagara Falls.❞
Maureen Paton (*Daily Express*)

❝Mr Dudley's set at first threatens to upstage the actors. They, however, are a resourceful and colourful assemblage of personalities who, under the expert direction of Howard Davies, soon assert themselves to great effect . . . Stephen Rea makes an engaging figure of the irrepressible Conn, whose wake at the beginning of Act III, after he has been shot by the police, provides the play's most hilarious scene. Stephen Moore is improbably but successfully cast as an eminently hissable villain.❞
Charles Osborne (*Daily Telegraph*)

❝The scene where we discover Kinchela in his dark Gothic den would surely have pleased an archshowman like Boucicault – Dudley has the room twirling up into view out of the glowing red sulphurous bowels of the Olivier stage. It is a classic way for a villain to arrive and the ritual boos that greeted it were really a form of cheering. This is a delightfully fresh and funny evening.❞
Christopher Edwards (*Spectator*)

CAST: Felicity Montagu (*Claire Ffolliott*), Gillian Barge (*Mrs O'Kelly*), Shaun Scott (*Captain Molineux*), Eve Matheson (*Arte O'Neal*), Stephen Moore (*Corry Kinchela*), Robert Urquhart (*Father Dolan*), Anthony O'Donnell (*Harvey Duff*), Fintan McKeown (*Robert Ffolliott*), Julia Dearden (*Moya*), Stephen Rea (*Conn, "The Shaughraun"*), Scamp (*Tatters*), Ged McKenna (*Sergeant Jones*), Kate Spiro (*Nancy Malone*), Philippa Howell (*Bridget Madigan*), Chris Dunne (*Donovan*), Michelle Evans, Marjorie Hogan, Alan White (*Keeners*), Mark Addy (*Reilly*), Paul Boyle (*Sullivan*), Toby E Byrne (*Mangan*), Robert Patterson (*Doyle*)
Musicians: Terry Davies, Tony Aldridge, Mark Emerson, Anthony Pike, Robert White, Carys Wyn Hughes
Director Howard Davies, *Settings* William Dudley, *Costumes* Liz da Costa, *Lighting* Mark Henderson, *Music* Dominic Muldowney, *Fights* Malcolm Ranson, *Falls and tumbles* Johnny Hutch, *Dialect coach* Joan Washington

1988 THE SHAUGHRAUN
by Dion Boucicault

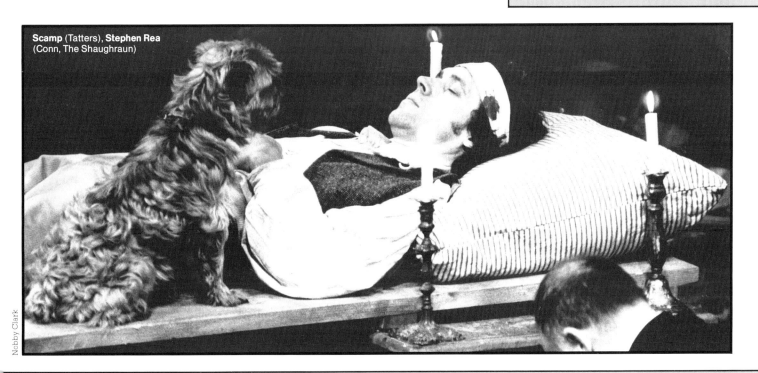

Scamp (Tatters), **Stephen Rea** (Conn, The Shaughraun)

Nobby Clark

1988

THE LATE SHAKESPEARES

CAST: Robert Arnold *(Cleomenes (WT), Alonso (T), Philario/2nd British Captain (C)),* Paul Ashby *(Gentleman (WT), Masque/Spirit (T), Soldier (C)),* Eileen Atkins *(Paulina (WT), Queen (C)),* Michael Beint *(Gaoler/Mariner (WT), Boatswain (T), 1st Goaler (C)),* John Bluthal *(Archidamus/3rd Gentleman (WT), Stephano (T), 1st Gentleman/1st Lord/Caius Lucius (C)),* Ian Bolt *(Attendant (WT), Masque (T), 2nd Gaoler (C)),* Michael Bottle *(First Lord/Gentleman (WT), Francisco/Masque (T), Roman Captain/Lord (C)),* Michael Bryant *(Old Shepherd (WT), Prospero (T), Soldier (C)),* Doyne Byrd *(Attendant/2nd Gentleman (WT), Masque (T), 2nd Brother/Attendant/1st Tribune (C)),* Michael Carter *(Time/Servant (WT), Adrian (T), 2nd Gentleman/2nd Lord/Jupiter (C)),* Tony Church *(Antigonus (WT), Gonzalo (T), Cymbeline (C)),* Judith Coke *(2nd Lady (WT), Masque (T), Lady-in-Waiting (C)),* Sally Dexter *(Hermione (WT), Juno (T)),* Jeremy Flynn *(Clown (WT), Arviragus (C)),* Jenny Galloway *(Mopsa (WT), Iris (T), Helen (C)),* James Goodwin *(Mamillius (WT)),* Peter Gordon *(Servant/1st Gentleman (WT), Masque (T), Cornelius/1st Senator (C)),* Jennifer Hall *(Dorcas (WT), Miranda (T)),* Alex Hardy *(Lord (WT), Masque (T), Messenger/1st Lord/1st Brother (C)),* Tony Haygarth *(Caliban (T), Pisanio (C)),* Shirley Henderson *(Perdita (WT), Masque (T)),* Basil Henson *(Camillo (WT), Sebastian (T), Belarius (C)),* Geraldine James *(Innogen (C)),* Steven Mackintosh *(Florizel (WT), Ariel (T), Guiderius (C)),* Tim Pigott-Smith *(Leontes (WT), Trinculo (T), Iachimo (C)),* William Puttock *(Mamillius (WT)),* Simon Scott *(Lord (WT), Masque (T), French Gentleman/Messenger/1st British Captain/2nd Senator (C)),* Ken Stott *(Autolycus (WT), Antonio (T), Cloten (C)),* Daniel Thorndike *(Officer of the Court (WT), Shipmaster (T), Soothsayer/Sicilius Leonatus (C)),* Janet Whiteside *(Emilia/1st Lady (WT), Masque (T), Lady/Mother to Posthumus (C)),* Peter Woodward *(Polixenes (WT), Ferdinand (T), Posthumus Leonatus (C))*

(WT) The Winter's Tale, *(T)* The Tempest, *(C)* Cymbeline

Director Peter Hall, *Designer* Alison Chitty, *Music* Harrison Birtwistle, *Lighting* Gerry Jenkinson and Ben Ormerod, *Movement* Elizabeth Keen, *Associate Director* Alan Cohen

Tim Pigott-Smith (Leontes)

John Haynes

❛Hall's great achievement is to weld a complicated narrative, a mixture of the earthy and the supernatural, philosophy and brutality, and a brisk but profound characterisation rather like the rapid, magisterial brush-strokes in Titian's late paintings, into an organic, breathing whole. It is done with an assurance, a miraculous consistency of tone, which are fully equal to these difficult, enchanting and profound plays. This is a majestic end to one of Hall's careers; now begins another. Let our indulgence set him free.❜ *John Peter (Sunday Times)*

THE WINTER'S TALE

❛Unlikelihoods and violent shifts of key and mood have no power to break the spell of some of Shakespeare's most sensuous verse. And the acting! . . . Virtually the entire cast could be singled out in turn. But the unseen star is the director, with his players creating Arcadian charms and country magic in Bohemia, intrigue and dark tragedy in Sicilia.❜ *Shaun Usher (Daily Mail)*

BARTHOLOMEW FAIR by Ben Jonson,
Dir. Richard Eyre, Olivier 20.10.88
MOUNTAIN LANGUAGE by Harold Pinter,
Dir. Harold Pinter, Lyttelton 20.10.88

Steven Mackintosh (Guiderius), Geraldine James (Innogen), **Jeremy Flynn** (Arviragus)

John Haynes

Steven Mackintosh (Ariel), **Michael Bryant** (Prospero)

THE TEMPEST

Instead of following *The Winter's Tale* as another magical romance, the sequel emerges as a Faustian revenge drama denuded of elegiac poetry and consoling reconciliations. Hall and his company have something fresh to say about this work and they go straight for the target in a high-energy performance running to just over two hours with no interval. The meaning is summed up in the figure of Bryant's Prospero: no longer a seraphic mage and unpolitical bookworm, but an impious magician devoured with hatred for the usurpers who have at last fallen into his power ... It is thrilling to witness this tortured human emerging from the anonymous shadow of stage tradition.
Irving Wardle (The Times)

CYMBELINE

A complex confrontation of virtue and vice, civility and degradation always shadowed by mortality: it is the *Into The Woods* of its day with everyone put on trial. Geraldine James's Innogen emerges superbly as a tough, strong-jawed woman full of irony and anger ... Hall's achievement is to suggest that *Cymbeline* is an epic play in which crucial human values are being put to the test.
Michael Billington (Guardian)

George Harris (De Flores),
Miranda Richardson (Beatrice-Joanna)

CAST: Paul Jesson *(Alsemero),* John Cassady *(Jasperino),* Paul J Medford *(First Servant),* Donald Campbell *(Second Servant),* Miranda Richardson *(Beatrice-Joanna),* George Harris *(De Flores),* Caroline Lee Johnson *(Diaphanta),* David Ryall *(Vermandero),* Stuart Golland *(Alibius),* Paul Barber *(Lollio),* Ivan Kaye *(Pedro),* Julian Wadham *(Antonio),* Mark Lockyer *(Alonzo de Piracquo),* Linal Haft *(Tomazo de Piracquo),* Rebecca Pidgeon *(Isabella),* Guy Henry *(Franciscus),* Trevor Marshall Ward *(Servant to Vermandero)*
Donald Campbell, Doreen Ingleton, Ivan Kaye, Douglas McFerran, Helen McGregor, Trevor Marshall Ward, Paul J Medford, Anthony Shirvell, Joanne Stoner *(Servants and Madpeople)*
Musicians: Ian Davies, Michael Gregory, Ramon Ruiz
Director Richard Eyre, *Designer* William Dudley, *Music* Dominic Muldowney, *Lighting* Mark Henderson, *Movement* Christopher Bruce

1988 THE CHANGELING
by **Thomas Middleton** and **William Rowley**

John Haynes

❝I know of no play so single-mindedly concerned with sex, not as the pursuit of pleasure but, at best, the visitation of "Love's tame madness".❞
Richard Eyre

❝As Beatrice-Joanna Miranda Richardson thrillingly tracks the zig-zagging of a woman trying to escape retribution by increasingly wild swervings . . . Deeply naive behind her little flurries of cunning, she glazedly clings to the belief – cruelly misplaced in Middleton's world – that even involvement in murder does not really change things. The play's most exciting scene shows her being horribly disabused of this notion by De Flores. Eschewing the conventional presentation of this "ill-faced" character, George Harris provides a grippingly original interpretation . . Combining unexpected subtlety and fierce energy, it is a performance finely representative of the qualities Eyre has brought to his production of this chilling play about feverish passions.❞
Peter Kemp (The Independent)

❝Richard Eyre's production, blending images of Goya horror with an atmosphere of Dali-like surrealism, shows again what an imaginative director can do with the kind of violent melo-drama that gripped audiences over 350 years ago.❞
Milton Shulman (Evening Standard)

❝Throughout, there is no embrace without fear, and passion is acted with an ardour that makes you feel you have never seen an embrace on stage before.❞
Kate Kellaway (The Observer)

GRAND NATIONAL

the NT as architecture

Within the NT are three separate and very distinct theatres. Symbolically and practically they are loosely modelled on theatre designs from the three greatest periods of western drama: the Olivier on classical Greek theatres, the Lyttelton on the proscenium-arch theatres of the past three centuries, and the Cottesloe on Tudor inn-yards.

The largest is the Olivier, named after Laurence Olivier, the first Director of the NT. It holds 1160 people in a fan-shaped auditorium,

Peter Hall with Denys Lasdun at the ancient theatre of Epidaurus, Greece. Its design is reflected in the shape of the Olivier auditorium

London Weekend Television

carefully designed to match an actor's effective span of vision, so that the whole audience can be held within the compass of his eyes. The stage is open, dispensing with the traditional proscenium arch and safety curtain. Under a ceiling of angled panels – to improve sound quality – and reflected lighting, two main tiers of steeply-raked seats, flanked by side banks on a higher level, sweep down to focus all attention on the stage. Although the circle has relatively few rows, so making sure no one is too far from the stage, it is able, because of the angle of the arcs of seats, to seat more people than the stalls.

Throughout the National, the walls are of shuttered concrete, roughly finished and bare of decoration.

The Lyttelton is a more or less conventional proscenium theatre. It holds 890 people in two straight tiers of seats which, by eliminating the central aisle, concentrate the audience in the best area for watching. As in the Olivier, the lighting, sound, and stage management and directors' control rooms are at the back of the stalls, and projection rooms with simultaneous translation booths (for use when foreign companies visit the theatre) are at the back of the circle. Unlike most traditional theatres, the Lyttelton has an adjustable proscenium: forestages can be added, the size of the arch itself altered, and an orchestra pit for 20 musicians can be made. It is possible to prepare

The Lyttelton foyer

The half-finished building in 1971. Somerset House is on the far side of the river, and Waterloo Bridge to the left

C W F Holmes

Denys Lasdun's office, packed with models of the NT

Behr Photography

complete sets behind soundproof doors, ready to slide on to the main stage at a moment's notice. The Lyttelton is named after Oliver Lyttelton, Viscount Chandos, first Chairman of the NT Board.

The smallest, barest and most flexible of the theatres is the Cottesloe. It is a rectangular room with two tiers of galleries looking down on an adjustable floor space. It holds from 200 to 400 people depending on the lay-out, and has been used in a wide variety of different ways, for NT productions and by visiting companies. It is named after Lord Cottesloe, Chairman of the South Bank Board – the body responsible for the construction of the National Theatre – and a former Chairman of the Arts Council.

The front-of-house area of the National has been designed to encourage people to relax and give them room to do so. The outside terraces continue inside, so there are many different levels on which people can listen to free live music, browse at one of the bookstalls, look at the exhibitions that are scattered over the building, have a drink or something to eat at one of the many bars and buffets, visit Ovations, the NT restaurant, or just simply sit and chat. The building has been planned as "the fourth auditorium", an area of casual encounter, where people provide their own entertainment as a backdrop to the theatres themselves. It is not just a theatre centre, it is a social centre, a theatre of the crowd.

At the time the building opened the architect said:

"It's in a magical position. Probably the most beautiful site in London. The two main theatres are signalled on the outside by two large blank concrete fly-towers. The bigger one, the Olivier, is inflected at an angle towards Waterloo Bridge and the smaller one, the Lyttelton, acts as a sort of point of stasis and is pretty well touching the bridge. The two towers are then tied as it were by a series of terraces, which step down towards the river, and symbolically and physically connect to the bridge.

"I call these terraces, which are very horizontal in emphasis, 'strata' – it's a geological term that rather goes with concrete – and these strata are available to the public to just mill around in. They are public places, public domains – an extension of the city. They furthermore penetrate into the building. This is entirely made up in a pyramidical form of the fly towers, the terraces, and the river front, and between these terraces is glass, so from the outside the people can be seen processing through the frame of the building.

"So the building itself is self-advertising. It is connected with the events of the world outside. It is not a temple with a door which says 'knock, come in' – it's already open.

"Nothing in this building has been disguised – it is what it is. And in a way this brings one to concrete, because a lot of people question the use of it.

"I think that concrete when you're using it at a domestic scale is very unfriendly – it's not a material that I would choose for a house – but we're dealing here with a major public building. It's a series of streets, terraces, strata. It is asymmetrical and it has its own dynamic. It is a sort of sculptural form that you can only do with reinforced concrete, but you need to work at a certain scale for this to come off. It's not a cosy little material.

"The rhythm of the building is interesting, given that it's by a river. Because I want the feeling that the audience – like the tides of the river – flow into the auditoriums and become a community within them. Then the tide ebbs and they come out into the creeks of the small spaces that are made by all these terraces; because they're not vast terraces, they are very small, human, little places for people to go to. Outside and inside."

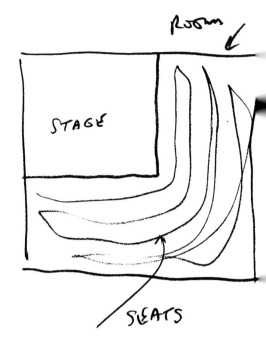

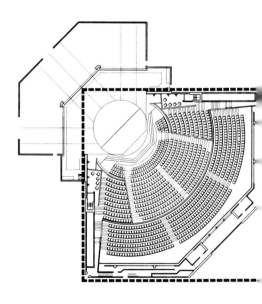

Denys Lasdun: "After listening to everybody for six months . . . I suddenly did a drawing. I said 'What you're all asking for is a room' – and I drew a square – 'and a stage in the corner'."

BACKSTAGE AND FRONT

working the NT

Theatre is a labour-intensive industry. The NT employs over 500 full-time staff, and roughly 100 actors – this number varying according to the repertoire.

Plays are chosen by the Directors of the NT, after discussion with colleagues. Every playscript sent in or suggested for performance is read and evaluated by the script department, and recommendations are made by the literary manager. There is also usually an NT writer-in-residence.

Once a play is decided upon, its director chooses his actors, helped by the casting department who see hundreds of actors every year.

Sets and costumes for the new show are designed; sometimes sets by one artist and costumes by another. The NT makes and keeps almost all its own costumes, which may be redesigned for use again in other productions, or hired out to other theatres. Wigs are hand-made.

When the play is ready for rehearsal, stage management organises and co-ordinates rehearsals and – later – performances. Each of the three NT theatres has a production manager working with the stage co-ordinator and workshops manager to link workshops and technical staff with the play's director. The production manager also helps to keep within a specific budget.

Most plays use music. There is a resident music director who composes the music for many but not all the productions, played by live musicians. Sometimes recorded music is selected.

To make a production takes many skills. The stage lighting department operate the lighting control boards, focus the hundreds of stage lighting units, changing them from one play to another, and manufacture all electrical additions, properties and scenery, for each production.

Music playback and sound effects are used in most productions and controlled from a sound desk. This department is responsible for every kind of sound effect on stage; recording music; relaying the shows and calls to actors in their dressing rooms; and general audio and video communications.

Basic stage settings are built outside the NT but everything else for a production is made in-house: scenic painting is done on the enormous paint frame; the armoury makes weapons, special effects, and certain props. In the property-making workshops almost anything can be – and is – constructed. Sometimes it is more economical to buy objects used in a play; this is the job of the property buying department.

For economy, too, after the run of a show the scenery is either used again in new forms for new sets or, wherever possible, sold. Props are kept for future use, or hired out.

Regular changeovers from one play to another mean there must be a large stage staff to take down and fit up the sets.

The NT administration includes house managers, responsible for the front-of-house areas of the theatre, the cleaning staff, the ushers, tours of the building, the information services – and the public. Also directly in touch with the public are the box office and the bookshops. The bars, buffets and restaurants are in the care of the catering department. There is separate staff for looking after exhibitions, platform performances, and the foyer music.

An essential part of theatre is publicity. People must be told what there is to be seen. The press office keeps TV, radio, newspapers and magazines informed, and suggests ideas to them. Illustrated programmes are published for every play. Theatre books, too, are published from time to time. The marketing department organises advertising, posters, leaflets, market research, ticket schemes and prices. In addition, it manages a network of NT sales representatives, and the NT mailing list. The graphics team design programmes and most promotional print. There is a special office to raise sponsorship.

The education department makes links with schools and colleges, and tours specially-created productions.

Touring at home and abroad of main house productions, and visits from other theatre companies to the NT, also require expert staff.

Other essential departments, common to all large organisations, are accounts, secretarial services, security, and maintenance.

A visually exciting broadsheet, *Making an NT Production*, is published by the NT and sold at the bookshops. It gives a vivid picture of how a production is created, plus much other detailed information.

SIGHTLINES

some views

‘The said National Theatre should be made to act as a great and true dramatic
school, at which alike the poet and the performer, the creator and the embodier (in
the highest walks of the dramatic and histrionic arts) should receive their diplomas,
living genius and talent being so fostered and sustained.’
Effingham Wilson (1848)

‘That such a theatre, as described, would be but worthy of this nation and would
not stand low upon the list of its instructors, I have no doubt. I wish I could cherish a
stronger faith than I have in the probability of its establishment within 50 years.’
Charles Dickens (1848)

‘There never was, and never will be, an ideal theatre. The theatre is too complex
and too delicate a machine, depending on the harmonious co-operation of too many
talents and influences, ever to reach perfection for more than a passing moment.
The very greatest theatres in their greatest periods have been severely criticized,
not, as a rule, without reason. The reader . . . will not fail to bear in mind, we trust,
that it is no magical recipe we are offering, no instant and miraculous cure for all the
shortcomings of our theatrical life.’
William Archer and Harley Granville Barker
(A National Theatre: Scheme and Estimates 1904)

‘The National Theatre must be its own advertisement, must impose itself on public
notice not by poster and column advertisements in the newspapers, but by the very
fact of its ample, dignified, and liberal existence.’
Archer and Granville Barker (1904)

‘I am one of those who hold that it is the duty of the State to be the generous but
discriminating parent of the arts and the sciences . . . Let us think with what excitement and interest we witness the construction and launching of a Dreadnought.
What a pity it is that some measure of this interest cannot be turned in the direction
of the launching, say, of a National Theatre.’
Winston Churchill (1906)

‘I want the State Theatre to be what St. Paul's and Westminster Abbey are to
religion – something to show what the thing can be at its best.’
Bernard Shaw (1930)

‘All this talk about a National Theatre. We *ARE* a National Theatre.’
Lilian Baylis at the Old Vic (*c.* 1930)

‘Do the English people want a national theatre? Of course they do not. They never
want anything. They have got the British Museum, the National Gallery and
Westminster Abbey, but they never wanted them. But once these things stood as

106

mysterious phenomena that had come to them they were quite proud of them, and felt that the place would be incomplete without them.
Bernard Shaw (1938)

Here lay we store, that at a future time
May bear a House, wherein, in days to be
Tier above tier, delighted crowds may see
Man's passions made a plaything and sublime.
John Masefield at the dedication of the foundation stone (1951)

At long last, after years of gestation, enough to put an elephant to shame, the National Theatre is about to be born.
Lord Esher (1955)

We need a National Theatre so badly. There is no theatre in this country at present where young people can see a repertoire of the great classics of the language. It is only in these great plays that the great tradition of theatre can be kept alive. I'm very worried for the younger generation. The theatre is in a very serious state of decline.
Donald Wolfit (1956)

Is it not clearer now than it has ever been before that no Government will give over £1 million for putting up a theatre the need for which is arguable?
The Manchester Guardian (1959)

Our aim is the best of everything.
Kenneth Tynan (1963)

If with £7,500,000 and an additional £100,000 we cannot build a splendid theatre, then we all ought to jump in the Thames.
Jennie Lee (1967)

It's the best theatre complex in the world that I have seen – there's everything you could possibly desire from the first idea to the opening night – you can store, make and rehearse everything under one roof.
Peter Hall (1973)

Our theatre generally is of enormous prestige value to our country . . . We once had a great reputation as a sporting nation, but we don't have that now. What we do have is an international reputation for the world of the arts. For drama, music, ballet, opera. The National Theatre ought to become the symbol of our achievements in the theatre.
Hugh Jenkins, Arts Minister (1974)

Like many a luxury, the National Theatre building may even turn out to have been a bargain. It will probably have cost about £16m, when all the bills are in and the other two theatres finished . . . and anything comparable, begun today, would cost from £25m to £40m.
The Economist (1976)

After all the sniping and griping, it is a relief to be able to report that the new

National Theatre feels not like a white elephant or cultural mausoleum: more like a superb piece of sculpture inside which it is possible to watch a play or walk and talk in the lobbies without feeling dwarfed by one's surroundings . . . my interim judgment on the new National . . . is that we have acquired a building in which . . . human need comes before architectural grandeur and in which everything conspires to make theatre-going a pleasure rather than a penance.
Michael Billington (*The Guardian*, 1976)

The massive new National Theatre . . . seems like the last glory of a troubled Britain, the final stronghold of her once imperial spirit . . . For Peter Hall this moment of crisis in British history is exactly the moment when Britain more than ever needs to call upon its cultural resources, and above all upon its theatre, which is without question the most varied and resourceful in the world.
Jack Kroll (*Newsweek*, 1976)

Britain now has the finest national theatre in the world; from that fact we must begin the discussion of it, to that fact we must return at the end, and that fact we must bear in mind throughout . . . Now, at last, we have not only a national theatre company, but a home worthy of it.
Bernard Levin (*The Times*, 1976)

Denys Lasdun's ambitious building has brought off a triumph to confound the sceptics. The huge foyer, which, with its tables and its Folies-Bergère Manet bars, with its people of all ages and classes walking up and down, listening to music, talking, creates an ambiance of social enjoyment that the French find it easy enough to evoke with their café tables spreading over the Paris pavements, but which has hitherto been unknown in London.
Harold Hobson (*The Sunday Times*, 1976)

One of the fascinating things about the National Theatre is the way it demonstrates how a public building can be designed as a setting for numbers of people; it's deliberately been made incomplete *without* people . . . I know of no other theatre where the audiences are given such a sense of being actors contributing to a festive occasion.
Sir James Richards (*Radio 3*, 1976)

I was proud of my position as the Director of the National, and always will be. And I'm certain that the work we did there was a great credit to the British theatre as a whole. I am convinced that, pound for pound, for a while we were the best troupe of players in the world. They were a sensational company, and they were a company in the true sense of the word. Any one of my team, at any time, could have taken the helm and steered a play into safe harbour. A wonderful company from the second assistant stage manager to the top. I felt I knew them all individually, and I think I did.
Laurence Olivier (*On Acting*, 1986)

You know what a reputation the National Theatre has, and when I walked in here the other day – and I've been here many times as an audience – I thought: the best things have come out of this place, and so I was a little awed. But once rehearsal starts, you're in any place.
Neil Simon (1986)

NATIONAL THEATRE BOARD MEMBERS 1962 to 1988

CHAIRMEN:
The Rt. Hon Viscount Chandos KG PC DSO MC (1962-71)
The Lord Rayne (1971-88)
The Lady Soames (1989-   )

Ronald Baird (1984-   )
Tony Banks (1981-84)
Hugh Beaumont (1962-73)
Caryl Brahms (1980-82)
Richard Brew (1982-85)
Nancy Burman (1965-69)
Timothy Burrill (1982-88)
Professor Raymond Carr (1968-76)
The Lord Chorley (1980-   )
Sir Kenneth Clark CH KCB (1962-67)
Sir Ashley Clarke GCMG GCVO (1962-66)
Rafe Clutton FRICS (1976-   )
Michael Codron (1988-   )
Professor Philip Collins (1976-82)
Freda Corbet JP MP (1962-65)
Sir Horace Cutler OBE (1975-82)
Alfred Francis OBE (1967-76)
Alderman Leslie Freeman OBE (1966-67)
George Geddes (1968-70)
John Hannam MP (1980-   )
Illtyd Harrington JP (1975-77)
Harvey Hinds (1973-85)
Sir Harold Hobson (1976-80)
Sarah Hogg (1988-   )
Hugh Jenkins MP (1976-80)
W J Keswick (1962-65)
Sir Ronald Leach CBE (1971-80)
Stuart Lipton (1988-   )
Sir Douglas Logan DCL LLD (1962-68)
Sonia Melchett (1983-   )
Richard M Mills (1976-   )

The Lord Mishcon DL (1964-   )
Sir Derek Mitchell KCB CVO (1977-   )
Yvonne Mitchell (1976-79)
Helen Montagu (1980-82)
Henry Moore OM CH (1962-67)
John Mortimer QC (1967-88)
The Rt. Hon. Lord O'Brien of Lothbury GBE PC (1973-78)
Sir Maurice Pariser (1965-68)
Sir Peter Parker LVO (1986-   )
Peter Pitt (1984-85)
The Lady Plowden (1976-88)
J B Priestley LLD (1965-67)
The Lord Rayne (1970-88)
Leopold de Rothschild (1968-70)
Derek Salberg JP (1962-65)
Peter Scott (1977-80)
Geoffrey Seaton (1977-81)
Harold H Sebag Montefiore (1968-80)
Lois Sieff (1980-   )
The Lady Soames (1988-   )
Professor Terence Spencer (1968-76)
Shaun Sutton (1970-73)
John Whitney (1982-   )
Hugh Willatt (1965-68)
The Lord Wilmot PC JP (1962-64)

SECRETARIES
Kenneth Rea (1962-74)
Douglas Gosling (1975-   )

ASSISTANT SECRETARY
Yolande Bird (1975-   )